Celebrate
CHRIST

Other Books by John Gillette:

Discovering God's Sufficiency
Going Beyond Ourselves and Experiencing the Supernatural
Pastoral Health Care — Part One

Discovering God's Love
Confirming God's Love through the evidence of historical facts
Pastoral Health Care — Part Two

Discovering God's Counsel
Applying his spiritual solution to meet difficult trials
Pastoral Health Care — Part Three

Discovering God's Kingdom
Finding a way to understand ourselves in a complex world
Pastoral Health Care — Part Four

Discovering God's Heart
Finding God's heart pulse is our daily challenge
Pastoral Health Care — Part Five

Glorify God
Christianity is a divine vitality
Divine Dialogue — Part One

Dynamic Doer
Biblical Christianity is Jesus Christ
Divine Dialogue — Part Two

Satisfying Strength
Biblical mediation works. Allow Psalms to sweep you into all directions
Divine Dialogue — Part Three

Positive Presence
Discovering God's presence in spiritual, psychological and physiological adjustments.
Divine Dialogue — Part Four

Above All Christ
—John 3:31

DIVINE
DIALOGUE
PART 5

Celebrate
CHRIST

"IF YOU HOLD ON TO MY TEACHING,
YOU ARE REALLY MY DISCIPLES.
THEN YOU WILL KNOW THE TRUTH,
AND THE TRUTH WILL SET YOU FREE."

JOHN 8:31-32

JOHN F. GILLETTE
Teaching Pastor
Pastoral Health Care Ministries

Chapbook Press

Schuler Books
2660 28th Street SE
Grand Rapids MI 49512

www.schulerbooks.com/chapbook-press

Distribution contact: jjgillette@comcast.net

ISBN 13: 9781957169002

Library of Congress Control Number: 2021924888

Cover photo: Pexels.com
Typist: Michael Sharp
Cover and Interior Layout: Frank Gutbrod Graphic Design

Printed in the United States of America

It is with great affection that I dedicate this book series to my wife, Joy, who radiates God's grace. We wrote the Pastoral Health Care Series together. Applying God's spiritual solutions to meet us in difficult trials has become even more practical in my life with the recent death of my dear wife, Joy. This book has been reproduced in her memory. While the content is the same, my dedication has become more personal than ever before. The separation is painful but as I gather my suffering and feelings of incompleteness, I will succeed with God's peace and presence. The guidelines of this book have brought blessing to our life together. We have pursued them with great persistence. I am assured that she is in God's presence, rejoicing and at peace. I will be with her to experience God's eternal presence someday as well.

" . . . blessed are they who put their trust in Him."

Psalm 2:12

Granddaughters of author

Aliya Joy Gillette

Jocelyn Joy Gillette

Technology & Celebration Helpers

Spiritual Solutions

A TEN-BOOK SERIES

Affirm

"Draw near to me and I will draw near to you"
(James 4:8).

Thinking right always precedes acting right. Spiritual insight and application will cause us to think right and act right. Put into action God's words (Matthew 5:1-12).

—Discovering God's Sufficiency

Accept

"People who know their God will display strength and take action" (Daniel 11:32).

"He that believeth on me" (John 7:38) has discovered God's love. Jesus has the same nature of God." "In the beginning was God" - Jesus Christ (John 1:1).

—Discovering God's Love

Adjust

"Jesus is the truth" (John 14:6).

I have confidence in Jesus. He is the final key to life. Fellowship is the key to hope. He says "I will never leave you nor forsake you" (Hebrews 13:5). My counsel comes from God (Psalm 1:1-2).

—Discovering God's Counsel

Apply

"Seek his kingdom" (Matthew 6:33).

His kingdom is a gift from God. Seek his kingdom, earthly and heavenly, and experience "you're Christ to me."

—Discovering God's Kingdom

Activate

"Make a melody in your heart to the Lord" (Ephesians 5:19).

Feeling God's heart pulse is our daily challenge. Reproduce the Bible in our lives. Meditation on the Scripture is the goal.

—Discovering God's Heart

Affirm

"Whatever you do, do it all for the glory of God" (1 Corinthians 10:31).

I have to mix his word with faith to glorify God (Hebrews 4:1-3). It involves knowledge and application of his word (James 1:22-24). Describe life with Matthew 5:1-12. God's Spirit will shine.

—Glorify God

Accept

"Be ye doers of the word . . ." (James 1:22).

Belief is based on believing and receiving the baptism of the Spirit by the "hearing of faith." Genuine faith is practice. His promises will produce victory. Relationship is a building process. Through God's grace faith will draw me closer to him.

—Dynamic Doer

Adjust

"I will instruct you" (Psalm 32:8).

Learning is the process of growth. Discipleship is a transforming process. It takes work, desire and goal-setting. It is a life-long achievement that never ends.

—Discipling Dynamics

Apply

"He is able to make all grace abound toward me" (2 Corinthians 9:8).

We have to decide to choose to follow God's plan. God has prepared for the way. We have to do something about it. Accept it, believe it, claim it and depend on it.

—Discovering God's Kingdom

Activate

"From withing him shall flow rivers of living water" (John 7:38).

We have to respond to scripture.

We have to rely on each promise.

We have to rest on God himself.

We have to repeat the process.

"If you remain in me and I in you, you will bear much fruit."

—Discovering God's Heart

Table of Contents

Introduction

JOHN 7:38

Prayer has taken me into a new dimension in my life. Through each transition of my spiritual autobiography, I have learned "not by might, not by power, but by my Spirit, saith the Lord of hosts" (Zechariah 4:6). It is God's work. He is fitting me through the enabling of the Holy Spirit. "God is able to make all grace abound toward men" (1 Corinthians 9:8). God's graciousness, goodness and greatness have led the way.

My life in Christ began with "Except a man be born of water and of the Spirit, he cannot enter into the kingdom of God" (John 3:5). I became a follower of Jesus Christ. The second part speaks of a full life: "whosoever drinketh of the water that I shall give him shall never thirst" (John 14:4).

The third thought speaks of an overflowing life: "from within shall flow rivers of living water"

(John 7:37-38). I hope to learn what it means to live in Christ and what it means to have Christ live in me and to bless others through that overflow. My life in Jesus Christ is a life to celebrate.

It all starts with activating these words: "He that believeth on me" (John 7:38). I can live with God's blessing flowing from within because I believe in Jesus Christ. He is deity. In all the gospels, it is spelled out in simple language. These expressions can only be spoken by God . . . Jesus said, "I am the truth, I am the way, I am the door, I am the bread, I am the life, I am the resurrection, I am the Messiah. I and the father are one." I believe it is possible because of who he is.

It follows with understanding who lives in me. "From within him shall flow rivers of living water" (John 7:38). The reception of the Holy Spirit through belief opens the door to his abundance. God will never give divine power in order that I may do my will. Divine power is always found in line with the divine purpose. The secret of power use is being in agreement with the divine will. The apostles have said that

God gives the Holy Spirit to them that obey him (Acts 5:32)). Obedience creates selflessness and selflessness requires reliance. God never gives power to store up for use. God is sovereign and it lies with him to determine the amount, the extent and the character of filling. The overflowing life must be asked for, believed in, claimed and received. (Luke 11:13; John 14;16,17).

As I learn to follow Jesus, life will become a celebration. I live in a day of desperation, discontent and depression. The negatives have led the way and have controlled the mind. The positives have been buried in the dust. I celebrate the fact that I have life in Jesus. As I learn his principles and practice them, life becomes a time spent with peace instead of desperation, guidance instead of discontent and confidence instead of depression. I have had to focus on a major theme from the Gospel of John. In each chapter, I have discovered a principle to live by. As I apply the instruction, a celebrated life becomes reality. It begins with the indwelling of the Holy Spirit through the acceptance of Jesus Christ into my heart. It involves communication, relationships, sufficiency, transformation, worship, belief, selection, conflict, justice, blindness, abundance, emotions, praise, love, comfort, remaining, prayer, intercession, crucifixion, resurrection and challenge.

Communications

JOHN 1:1-14

Life becomes a celebration as I learn to follow Jesus. I have decided to review the Gospel of John and discover what was characterized in his daily life. I have preached through the gospel written by John several times. No matter what my soul needs — comfort, encouragement, conviction or challenge. It will be found in the fourth gospel. I want to change. I want to allow Jesus Christ to live through me. I know it is only in trusting through Christ that I can have eternal life, experience his transforming power and overflow within his grace.

Jesus Christ is the ultimate personality of the universe. "In the beginning" (John 1:1) refers to eternity which preceded all time. Jesus always was. This gives evidence that Jesus has the same attributes as God. The word "with" in the text

(1:1) implies association. He is a living intelligent active personality. Jesus Christ the 'Word' has the same character of God, the same work and the very nature of God. He is deity.

Jesus Christ is in partnership with God. "All things came into being through him." This relates to the universe, its elements and its system of law. Christ is the agent through whom deity expressed itself. The earth owes its origin to God through the work of Jesus.

Jesus Christ is the life. This refers not only to conscious existence but of the life of God. Spiritual vitality originates with God and that lifts man out of sin to himself. Christianity is the indwelling of God into our everyday activities. Jesus Christ is the light and through him, I am given spiritual illumination. He is the original light. He is the source. The word 'world' has reference to the material and spiritual environment in which we live. He is independent of it and yet a part of it. The only way I can comprehend is through believing and then he gives understanding. I have discovered Jesus Christ is God. As I read verses 1 and 2, I realized that they are connected to verse 14. In verses 1 and 2, they speak of the eternal nature and relation of Jesus Christ to God and verse 14 connects him with the world of men. God has expressed himself in human personality that was visible, audible and tangible. He partook of flesh. He belongs to humanity as well as to infinity.

The phrase "dwelt among us" means that Jesus Christ camped among us. His stay was temporary but not illusory. God has come into our daily life. When observation, confession and personal appropriation of the truth takes place, he becomes my live-in companion.

No one has ever seen God. The "only begotten God" are words of affirmation that Jesus is deity. He is the revelation of God. Either I accept or reject this truth. Receiving and believing are equivalent terms. Receiving Jesus Christ and believing bring us into a relationship with God and his family. Belief gives the authority to place us into his family. Jesus Christ communicated

God to man. I want to be a witness for Jesus and communicate how humanity can have a relationship with God. I want to be an extended light for him. A celebrated life involves communicating God to men.

Dear Heavenly Father,

I pray that I might be a good communicator of the faith. Jesus not only is creator of all things but has blazed the way with the light that cannot be put out. I pray for an honest, bold and fearless witness. Help me to communicate God to everyone I come in contact with.

I love you. Amen

Relationships

JOHN 1:1-15-51

Life becomes a celebration as I learn to follow Jesus. As I contemplate Chapter One on the gospel of John, I have learned what is required in making relationships. In John the Baptist's words, "Behold the Lamb of God," the first followers of Jesus takes place. The words, "the Lamb of God" refer to the Messiah, which means the anointed one, or Christ. Relationships are developed through an introduction to someone with a common interest. This can lead into a desire for fellowship. It will put a person into a position of deliberate conversation. Action will turn to an invitation of others to develop a relationship. The inner motivation involves the challenge, "Thou art . . . thou shall be."

A relationship may begin with an invitation or the seeking of a relationship. It may be a willing, silent response or an outspoken objective. In either case, the challenge of a progressive possibility of belief should take place. Sometimes relationships can take place in a quiet time of meditation and sometimes it may take place in a festive occasion. Sensitivity to the Holy Spirit and discernment is necessary. Jesus' credentials are found in his words, "My Father" which relates him to God. My credentials are given through the Holy Spirit.

New relationships bring freshness to life. In building relationships, the desire is to be open and transparent. Andrew followed Jesus and became the first missionary. He enjoyed a special friendship with Jesus. I need to have the same passion to lead others to Christ like Andrew. Peter followed Jesus and became immovable in his convictions. He failed and yet was restored and became a dauntless leader of the church. I need to have the same convictions like Peter to lead in the church. Philip did not approach Jesus but waited for an invitation. He was not afraid to share his faith even though he made some mistakes. I need to have the readiness for action like he did. Nathaniel was honest and straightforward. He was also skeptical but curious. In his story, I am challenged to realize that Jesus is always working on people's hearts. Am I ready to be his representative? A celebrated life involves making relationships.

Dear Heavenly Father,
I am a loner. I don't mind being alone. I cherish quiet times of meditation. This does not mean I can't be sociable. I mix very well in groups and usually start the conversations. I must use my sensitivity and discernment to reach out to people. I realize building relationships are important. The church is a place of relationships. When God created man, he didn't want him to be alone. I want to be more alert to the needs of others and not just my own. I am praying my books will tell my story as I communicate God and develop relationships. I pray that my sensitivity and discernment will be helpful in making relationships. I realize you did not create man to be alone. Help me to follow your example and build solid relationships. I love you. Amen.

Personal Response

1. What has the chapter taught me? *(Overview)*

2. What level of commitment do I have in this study? *(Attitude)*

3. Who is my reliable resource? *(Confidence)*

4. What spiritual transformation have I learned? *(Discipleship)*

5. Have I experienced spiritual illumination? *(Enlightenment)*

6. What does the word "light" mean in this chapter? *(Understanding)*

7. Will I put the principal found in the chapter into prayer and practice it? *(Relationship)*

8. Will I share what I have learned in the chapter? *(Communication)*

CHAPTER TWO

Sufficiency

JOHN 2:11

Life becomes a celebration as I learn to follow Jesus. After I trusted in Jesus and began to worship him, I found that he was sufficient in all things because he is sovereign. I am learning that his grace works. He says, "my grace is sufficient" (2 Corinthians 12:9). I can rely upon his word. As I walk in the Lord and the Holy Spirit, I will experience his grace. His grace will help me in time of need (Hebrews 4:10). How does God's grace work in me? The process is found in 1 Peter 5:10 . . . "after you have suffered a little while he will restore you, make you strong, firm and complete."

His grace is sufficient. His grace is seen through each of these words. It is all possible because a sovereign God is behind it all. He will restore me. This means that he is working on me.

He is perfecting me. He is making me complete. Every day I must be reminded that his armor will protect me. I must keep in mind that the entire 'trinity' is working on my behalf. His word says be strong in the Father, be mighty in the Son, and be powerful in the Spirit (Ephesians 6:1). I am confident because I have entrusted my body, soul and spirit to my sovereign, sufficient God. In all circumstances, he is in charge. He gave his Son for me. I am worth something to him. Praise God for his unmerited favor.

I am not only confident because of his promise of restoration but he has promised to establish me. He helps me to hold my ground. He is my defense and will preserve me. He will help me and keep me safe. I will not deny him, compromise or be shamed. I am learning to be firm, to persevere and to be optimistic.

He not only gives me defensive weapons to keep a solid foundation but has promised strength. The strength provides offensive strategy. I will resist in his name. I will understand the enemy's deceptive ways. I will keep in fellowship. I will claim his promises to encircle me. I have to learn to rest in these promises and act on them daily.

God will mold me, establish me, strengthen me and settle me. I can rest in him because he has planned it all out. God is the sovereign, sufficient one. I am secure in him because his grace is upon me. I don't deserve it but I am thankful for it. As I face life's difficulties and pleasures, I am learning to depend on him. I am learning to let go of self and respond to His word.

As I experience his grace in my life, I am reminded of his miracles. They prove that he can do what he has promised to do. The miracles of Jesus confirm his nature, teaching and claims. They are a logical expression of his deity.

Did you hear about how Jesus saved a family from social embarrassment? I am sure you have heard about the water being changed to wine. Wine was the normal drink of the people in that day. The Jews diluted the wine with water. The purpose of the miracle is not about alcoholic beverages. Jesus accepted invitations to social events. He entered into the normal experience of life. Jesus had a heavenly timetable for everything. We can trust Jesus to do what is right and the miracle was for a few to witness: Mary, the disciples and the servants. This act of kindness revealed Jesus' glory (1:14) and gave a strong foundation to faith. Faith will become deep as you get to know Jesus. Have you experienced his grace in your faith walk?

Did you hear about the father that came to Jesus to intercede for his son who was dying? It does not make any difference who you are, whether noble, rich, poor, educated or uneducated, an official or a servant. The father was in desperate need. He believed in the words of Jesus and acted on them. The boy was healed the instant that Jesus spoke, "thy son liveth." Have you been in a crisis in your faith and experienced God's grace? We believe in a God that can heal and provide grace.

Did you hear about the man that was sick for thirty-eight years? He spent his days at a pool that would produce hope for healing of his infirmities. Jesus' grace was seen through his coming to the man, speaking to the man, healing the man and then visiting him later in the temple. We certainly see a tragic hopeless case. The cure was immediate. It happened through the power of his spoken word. What hopeless situation are you at in your faith? Has God's grace been experienced?

Did you hear about the feeding of the five thousand? Jesus faced a huge problem. What was he going to do with all those people? The need was food. They needed to have strength to travel back home after hearing him speak. We learn through bad and good things that happen to us. One of the disciples found a little boy who had a small lunch. Jesus took the boy's lunch, blessed it, broke it and handed it out to his disciples and they fed the whole crowd. Jesus multiplied the food. Whenever there is a need, give all that you have to Jesus and let him do the rest. Are we thankful to Jesus for the provision he has provided? Do not complain about what you don"t have but be thankful for what you do have. Let your eyes see his grace at work.

Did you hear about the storm? Sometimes we are caught in a storm of our own making because we have disobeyed Jesus. Sometimes storms come because we have obeyed the Lord.

We can be sure that our Savior will pray for us, come to us and deliver us. Jesus walked on the water and he stilled the storm and the boat was instantly on the other shore. I wonder how many people want Jesus as Savior and Lord. How many people want Jesus as healer and provider? How many people want Jesus to rescue them from problems? When the storms of life have come, have you witnessed his grace?

Did you hear about the man what was blind? I am told that in the United States somebody goes blind every twenty minutes. His eyes were opened to see but most importantly, his heart was opened to the Savior. He was born blind. He had never seen the beauty of God's creation on the faces of his loved ones. He was a beggar by trade. Jesus Christ is God but he is also man. The blind man becomes a witness for Jesus Christ's claims. He discovered that Jesus came for salvation but the result of his coming was condemnation of those who would not believe. His grace makes it possible for me to believe.

Did you hear about Jesus raising somebody from the dead? The person was in the grave four days. Death is man's last enemy, but Jesus Christ has defeated this horrible enemy totally and permanently. In every miracle there is a human need met and a spiritual truth delivered. His credentials prove his deity. There is no guarantee that we will be sheltered from the problems and pains of life. Jesus is the master of every situation. We must live by faith and not by sight. In Psalm 5:1-3 we find a great promise. Look it up and memorize it. God's grace is seen. Spiritual growth is not automatic. In Jesus' miracles, we are taught to believe his Word. The grace of God provides the way for us to live it out.

The miracles have given evidence of his power. The promises have revealed his grace in action. I am sufficient in all things because of Jesus Christ. Whatever the past, present or future brings into my life, I will experience his grace. A celebrated life involves his sufficiency.

Dear Heavenly Father,

I am walking with a smile and tears when I think about your graciousness directed toward me. I have so many blessings. Even the hardships have drawn me closer to you. This brings a new dimension in my relationship with you. Help me to shine brightly, not with a dim light, but like a spotlight. My life must demonstrate your promises that have been produced through your grace in me. Sufficiency in my daily life is possible because of your sovereignty. Thank you,
I love you. Amen.

Personal Response

1. What has the chapter taught me? *(Overview)*

2. What level of commitment do I have in this study? *(Attitude)*

3. Who is my reliable resource? *(Confidence)*

4. What spiritual transformation have I learned? *(Discipleship)*

5. Have I experienced spiritual illumination? *(Enlightenment)*

6. What does the word "light" mean in this chapter? *(Understanding)*

7. Will I put the principal found in the chapter into prayer and practice it? *(Relationship)*

8. Will I share what I have learned in the chapter? *(Communication)*

CHAPTER THREE

Transformation

JOHN 3:1-21

Life becomes a celebration as I learn to follow Jesus. This is impossible without a relationship with him. Jesus had several conversations in the following verses. They were from different experiences, education, interest and cultures. His conversation had a special topic of interest. He always adapted his discussion to fit the person he was talking to. I am going to give our Savior's explanation for spiritual transformation. If I am going to characterize Jesus, I must have Jesus in my life.

Spiritual transformation involves believing in not only the miracles or signs that Jesus performed to give authenticity to his person but a full acceptance of his claims and commands. Jesus knows if we believe or not. He knows the heart of man and can evaluate our faith. What is spiritual transformation? It is the internal change (2 Corinthians 5:17) of a person's nature through God's grace. Faith is the process for Jesus to enter and dwell in our hearts (Ephesians 3:17). There should be no confusion, camouflage, cover-up or stumbling.

In Jesus' own words, he declares what the gospel is all about and gives us an explanation. He says that we cannot enter the kingdom of God without becoming a new person. A complete change is compared to a rebirth. The natural man cannot enter into God's kingdom. The word in the text "cannot" implies incapability rather than prohibition. Spiritual transformation has to take place. How can change take place? The pattern of life is set. Physical or psychological change is not the question. It has to do with the spiritual side of man. Jesus gives these words, "except one be born of water and the Spirit, he cannot enter into the kingdom of God." In the word "water," I discovered that acknowledgement of repentance and cleansing is necessary. A complete turnaround in body, soul and spirit is necessary. To explain the word "Spirit," Jesus illustrates by using the word "wind." The wind origin is undiscoverable but whose presence is manifested. Nobody can deny its existence. To be born by the Spirit means that the origin of life cannot be defined but its actuality can be seen by all.

How do I experience this new nature? Jesus continues and says that new birth is a direct result of faith in his death and resurrection power. Jesus gives God's attitude and purpose toward the world. He "loved us" are words of the will rather than emotion. Belief is obedience to the voice of God; disobedience is unbelief. Belief is defined as commitment to authority rather than passive opinion.

We can come to Christ as a learned inquirer. We can come in an attitude of indifference. We can come as a result of desperation. Accept God's love and place your trust in his Son and be spiritually transformed. A celebrated life involves spiritual transformation.

Dear Heavenly Father,

Thank you for making it possible for me to come to you through Jesus Christ. It seems impossible that I am talking to my creator, redeemer, and sustainer for life. I believe you and love you. Thank you for my spiritual transformation.

I love you, Amen.

Personal Response

1. What has the chapter taught me? *(Overview)*

2. What level of commitment do I have in this study? *(Attitude)*

3. Who is my reliable resource? *(Confidence)*

4. What spiritual transformation have I learned? *(Discipleship)*

5. Have I experienced spiritual illumination? *(Enlightenment)*

6. What does the word "light" mean in this chapter? *(Understanding)*

7. Will I put the principal found in the chapter into prayer and practice it? *(Relationship)*

8. Will I share what I have learned in the chapter? *(Communication)*

Worship

JOHN 4:24

Life becomes a celebration as I learn to follow Jesus. In Jesus' conversation with the Samaritan woman, he gives the true definition of worship. It is found in her heart relationship with God. Many things can be said about this conversation. Much time could be spent on the words, "He must needs pass through Samaria." The use of the word "must" is not based on geographical necessity nor social pressure but a compulsion to seek a lost sheep. The time of day was important. Jesus would be weary and ready to rest. His request was a complete surprise. He asked someone for water that was his worst enemy. Jews and Samaritans did not mix together. Jesus gets into the spiritual side of the conversation which was water that is ties to eternal life. He turned her life inside out before her very eyes. He said that to worship God must be done through his Spirit and on the basis of truth. In his conversation with the woman, he would overcome the obstacles of indifference, materialism, selfishness, moral sin and religious prejudice, ignorance and indefiniteness. Through it all, he led her straight to the beginning of an active faith.

In my study of this scripture, I was challenged to worship with the right attitude. The Samaritans took as much of scripture as they wished and paid no attention to the rest. I have discovered that one of the most dangerous things in the world is a one-sided Christianity. It is very easy to accept and hold to certain truths that suit us and disregard the rest. I think to worship in the right way requires that I know what I believe and why I believe it. In this passage, I found these profound words, "God is a spirit and they that worship him must worship him in spirit and in truth" (John 4:24). This is very important to me because it will take me from the present to eternity and eternity to an unending life with Jesus Christ. It will become a Holy Spirit stimulated vitality.

Worship requires approaching God with the whole person. The emotional response is important but that response has to be thought out. My hope is built on solid ground. Real faith is not founded on fear of what might happen if we leave God out of the picture of life. It is a love for God in gratitude for what he has done.

Worship requires the spirit of man to be motivated. The other parts (physical, psychological) will vanish. It is through my spirit that I become intimate with God. True worship is not to come to a certain place. It is not to go through a certain ritual. It is not even to bring certain gifts. It is when my invisible part meets with God. It may be beyond my understanding and it may be full of wonder and amazement.

Worship requires love. The Bible says, "Love the Lord your God with all your heart and with all your soul and with all your mind" (Matthew 22:37-38). Jesus Christ becomes the priority in life. My entire being is activated.

Worship requires spending time with God. I must focus on him. Am I God-conscious? He is always conscious of me. He will never leave me nor forsake me (Deuteronomy 31:6). I initiate God-consciousness through praying, praising, reading the Bible, thoughtful meditation, etc.

Worship requires a choice. I must be in the right relationship with God. He says, "Be still and know that I am God" (Psalm 46:10). My response is to turn to him in total submission and reliance.

Worship requires sensitivity to God. Have I practiced the presence of God? Am I developing communion with God that has been established through my union with Jesus? A celebrated life involves worship.

Dear Heavenly Father,
I pray that my worship will always stem from my heart. I am glad that I worship in truth and spirit. You have made this possible. Help me to practice your presence. Please accept my humble worship.
I love you. Amen.

Personal Response

1. What has the chapter taught me? *(Overview)*

2. What level of commitment do I have in this study? *(Attitude)*

3. Who is my reliable resource? *(Confidence)*

4. What spiritual transformation have I learned? *(Discipleship)*

5. Have I experienced spiritual illumination? *(Enlightenment)*

6. What does the word "light" mean in this chapter? *(Understanding)*

7. Will I put the principal found in the chapter into prayer and practice it? *(Relationship)*

8. Will I share what I have learned in the chapter? *(Communication)*

CHAPTER FIVE

Belief

JOHN 5:24

Life becomes a celebration as I learn to follow Jesus. He said, "All that the Father giveth me shall come to me." This refers to God's sovereignty in my salvation (Romans 8:29-30). He continues in saying ". . . and him that cometh to me" (Ephesians 1:3-6). This is my responsibility to respond. Then he ends the invitation with a guarantee: "I will in no wise cast out." I have been chosen by the Father, purchased by the Son and sealed by the Holy Spirit (Ephesians 1).

The process begins with belief; ". . . everyone who sees the Son and believes in him" (John 6:40). God works through faith and faith is provided as a gift (Romans 12:3; Ephesians 2:8,9). Listen to what Jesus has to say . . . don't murmur or become hardened in the heart. Keep a clear perspective and mind-set. My heart was opened through his

Word. His Word actually penetrated my mind, will and emotion.

Believing involves faith (2 Peter 1:1). When I believed in Jesus (John 1:12), I received the gift of faith (Ephesians 2:8-9). Faith is the ability to choose fellowship with God, to bey him, to love him, and to acknowledge him in all areas of life through complete submission and aggressive trust.

Through faith I have been forgiven (Acts 26:18). I have a living relationship with God (Romans 1:17). I have been justified (Romans 5:1). I have a life indwelt by God (Galatians 2:20).

Faith is personal and is based on the character of the one I believe (Romans 4:17-21). It is not based on emotion or circumstances. It accepts the promises of God as true and interprets them on the basis of the attributes of God.

My personal salvation was a response to God and is based on who he is (Matthew 9:28-29; John 1:2). It was easy for me to trust Jesus because he is God. The miracles and his claims have brought me into his family. He said, "I am the bread of life."

Jesus is able to give life and sustain it. My hunger and thirst has been fully satisfied through him. My relationship with God includes trust, intimacy, obedience and love. Without Jesus, life is only an existence. I had to receive or reject his invitation.

Jesus said, "I am the light." As each year in my life slips by, I see more darkness and sin around me. In this world of depression, I have discovered that Jesus shines as the light. Jesus is the very light of God that has come among his creation. Jesus is the guide and means to understanding life and direction.

He said, "I am the door." Jesus is the entrance into God's family. Through him I have access to a life that God wants me to have. On one hand, he offers safety and the other security. I am thankful that I have gone through that door and have experienced new life and vitality.

He said, "I am the Good Shepherd." Jesus gave his life for me in my behalf and for my benefit. He is a gracious shepherd that provides for everything I need. He is efficient, skillful and kind. He loves me and cares for me. He is aware of my necessities before I am.

His quality of care is beyond compare. He is indeed a good shepherd: "the Lord is my shepherd, I shall not want." (Psalm 23). He said, "I am the resurrection." Jesus not only takes care of my temporal earthly needs but more importantly, he provides eternal life. I think the bottom line to all he says and the basis for absolute truth is the resurrection. I have placed my trust on that truth. I have been set free — no more frustration or futile living.

He said, "I am the way." He says come and I will take you. You cannot miss the way because I am the way. He is not only giving advice, direction and counsel. He is the way. He takes me by the hand and leads me . . . personally (Psalm 27:11).

He said, "I am the truth." I have confidence because moral perfection finds its realization in him. He is the final key to life. He speaks with final authority in words adapted to human understanding (Psalm 86:11).

He said "I am the life." The way was a means of reaching the Father. The truth defined the righteous standards of the way. The life originated with God and lifts me out of my sin to him. "In him was life and the life was the light of man" (John 1:4). "Christianity is the impartation of a divine vitality." "I am indwelt by the Spirit of God" (Psalm 16:11).

He said, "I am the true vine." He is real and genuine. Jesus is the source of the heavenly life. All the "I am's" point to the authority that is found in Jesus Christ. He is the only solid foundation to build upon. It is a must to abide in him. This means unbroken connection is maintained. It is the necessity of a constant active relationship between me and my Lord. Obedience to Christ will produce fruit. "By their fruits you shall know them" (Matthew 7:16). I believe in the death and resurrection of Jesus Christ for my sin and justification with God. A celebrated life involves belief.

Dear Heavenly Father,
Thank you for making a way to be saved from your wrath and judgement. I would never want to be separated from you. I know you are holy, pure and

perfect. Thank you for preparing a way through Jesus Christ to enter your kingdom and to have my sins forgiven. I believe that this is a personal relationship based on belief and is provided through faith. Than you Lord for saving my soul. Thank you for making me whole.

I love you. Amen

Personal Response

1. What has the chapter taught me? *(Overview)*

2. What level of commitment do I have in this study? *(Attitude)*

3. Who is my reliable resource? *(Confidence)*

4. What spiritual transformation have I learned? *(Discipleship)*

5. Have I experienced spiritual illumination? *(Enlightenment)*

6. What does the word "light" mean in this chapter? *(Understanding)*

7. Will I put the principal found in the chapter into prayer and practice it? *(Relationship)*

8. Will I share what I have learned in the chapter? *(Communication)*

CHAPTER SIX

Selection

JOHN 6:65

Life becomes a celebration as I learn to follow Jesus. When I was a little boy, I sang in a trio. A favorite song discovered for us to sing was entitled, "His Very Own." It had three major phrases in it. They would provide three short solos for the triplets which were "chosen by the Father, purchased by the Son and sealed by the Spirit." I am grateful that I have been chosen. This doesn't mean that I merit it and I have not done one thing to achieve it. Through God's grace, I have received Jesus Christ as my Savior.

The Bible says, "And he said, Therefore I said unto you, that no man can come unto me, except it were given to him of my Father." (John 6:65). Saving faith is a gift of God. My growing faith continues to be solid. Where else will I turn? Jesus has the words of eternal life. My conviction is found in the fact that he is "the holy one of God." (John 6:68-69). There is none other that demands my respect and reverence. Believing indicates and existing state resulting from a completed act. It is a settled fact that is fixed in my heart. It is more than an act of the will or decision of the mind. It is a spiritual union brought about by God himself.

As I began to read through the Gospel of John, I found several verses to verify this truth. Sometimes I think I would like to say that I chose to follow Jesus. I did but it puts more authority to the subject if I can say that God the Father chose me instead. I became aware of God and his call through the Scriptures, my parents, church leaders, books, songs and preachers. My heart-emotions and mind-will made a decision to trust Jesus Christ. I may not understand but I do nor really have to. It's who I have trusted that counts. "Ye have not chosen me but I have chosen you." (John 15:16,17).

I have been enslaved to sin (total depravity) and unable to believe apart from God's empowerment. (Romans 3:1-19; Ephesians 2:1-3; 2 Corinthians 4:4; 2 Timothy 1:9). It is through

God's drawing power that I have received Jesus Christ. I have chosen to come to Jesus and God will not turn me away (Romans 10:11-13). The absolute sovereignty of God is the basis of Jesus confidence. It is also my guarantee and security of salvation. In his sovereignty, I have been drawn to him. My responsibility in salvation is to believe through faith. God's responsibility is to draw me to him. The infinite mind of God is at work if I understand it or not. The Father has given certain people to Jesus Christ. How do I find out if I am one of them? The answer is by coming to Jesus. I have free will and can choose to come, and I have Jesus' words that he will not turn me away.

God the Father not only created me but has a plan for my life. A part of his work was to impress upon my heart to come to him. "This is the work of God, that ye believe in him whom God hath sent." (John 6:29). The work is not something I do for God but it is the act of receiving what God has done for me. I have discovered eternal life through accepting Jesus personally and his claims.

My whole personality played a part in the decision to follow Jesus. My intellect, will and emotion were moved by the Holy Spirit to choose. It was ultimately his will that made it happen. ". . . the Son giveth life to whom he will." (John 6:29). I am so thankful that the prodding of the Spirit was active in my life. It was God's will that I would become a believer.

It may be a mysterious statement but it is also an encouraging truth. When the Scripture says, "Those whom the Father gave him shall come to him." (John 6:37a). The work of the father and his will and the power of the Son brings meaningfulness to life. "Salvation of God is not of him that willeth nor of him that runneth, but of God that hath mercy." (Romans 9:16). Salvation involves both divine sovereignty and human responsibility. The Father gives men and women to the Son but these men and women must come to him, that is, believe on him. There is no conflict in God's perspective.

Jesus died for the world (John 3:16; 6:51), for his sheep (John 10:11-15), for the nation (John 11:50-52) and for his friends John 15:12). Jesus is the sacrifice not for our sins only but also for the sins of the whole world (1 John 2:2). I am glad that I have heard his call and have come to him. A celebrated life involves his selection.

Dear Heavenly Father,
Thank you for calling me into your kingdom. I realize that I don't merit your invitation. Since my childhood, I have followed you. I know saving faith is a gift. I may not understand it all, but I have an inner witness of assurance that I belong.
I love you. Amen.

Personal Response

1. What has the chapter taught me? *(Overview)*

2. What level of commitment do I have in this study? *(Attitude)*

3. Who is my reliable resource? *(Confidence)*

4. What spiritual transformation have I learned? *(Discipleship)*

5. Have I experienced spiritual illumination? *(Enlightenment)*

6. What does the word "light" mean in this chapter? *(Understanding)*

7. Will I put the principal found in the chapter into prayer and practice it? *(Relationship)*

8. Will I share what I have learned in the chapter? *(Communication)*

CHAPTER SEVEN

Conflict

JOHN 7:17

L ife becomes a celebration as I learn to follow Jesus. In the last six months of Jesus' life, he faced many conflicts. It is the longest single section in the Gospel of John. It describes the development of belief and unbelief among the hearers of Jesus. It represents fixed attitudes at war with one another and not just unsettled attitudes. The conflicts include unbelief of the brethren (John 7:3-9), the bewilderment of the people (John 7:10-13), public appearance (John 7:14-19), public confusion (John 7:20,25-32), offer of spiritual life (John 7:37-52), women taken in adultery (John 7:53-8:11), and address to the Pharisees (John 8:12-30).

Interpersonal tension surrounds everyday living. I have observed strife, jealousy, angry tempers, disputes, slanders, gossip and arrogance

(2 Corinthians 12:21,22). The Bible shares breakdowns starting with Adam and Eve, the first married couple, and their first two sons. As I traveled through the Scriptures, there were many. Jesus and the Biblical writers were peacemakers. I would like to know how I can be a peacemaker. It starts with Jesus. Peace with God comes when we confess our sins and failure to him, ask him to take control of our lives and expect that he will give the peace which the Word of God promises.

It includes growing in grace and becoming spiritually minded which means yielding to divine control. I have been transformed within and that makes an outward change in my behavior. Resolving conflicts involves determination, effort and skill. It is not just going to happen automatically. It demands desire, consistent development and application of such skills as listening carefully, watching, understanding oneself and others, refraining from unkind comments or emotional outbursts and communicating accurately.

I have learned that I have to will to do his will. "If any man will do his will." (John 7:17c). I can handle conflicts in light of his will. I cannot judge on the surface level. "Judge not according to the appearance; it must flow from within with divine direction." (John 7:38). This brings me to a spiritual test. If I pass, I will do alright and if I don't, I must continue to develop through God's grace. The spiritual reality test is based on the elements that are the fruit of the Spirit. Do I display in character the nine elements that make up the fruit? If I am aware of the need to be sensitive, determined, anxious and obedient, I will respond to conflicts in the way Jesus did.

Love must be major in any lifestyle. It is a deliberate act based upon my relationship to Jesus. I have as a top priority to become intimate with Jesus. He is my best friend and companion. He is also my God and creator. I am determined because of this relationship to display sacrifice and benevolence to others. Love brings joy into my life. I can live with contentment in all situations because the one I love is in charge. Satisfaction will fill my spirit, soul and body. It's built upon God's promises that I rely upon daily. With this foundation, I have inner joy. A sense of sacrifice and happiness is the result.

Inner love and joy will produce peace. I can rest in all circumstances. God is with me. He lives in me. I may not understand such knowledge. It it beyond me but I accept through faith. I am conscious of God's presence and this brings tranquility in my heart. In my relationship with Jesus, I have a sense of sacrifice, happiness and rest.

My relationship with God the father and the Son will change my relationship with humanity. It is through the Holy Spirit that I can be characterized with patience, kindness and goodness. He gives me an enduring power to deal with people that are not so easy to help. My attitude can change for the better. I can look deep into the situations with discernment. Personal steadfastness will accompany my acts of goodness. It becomes real through God's grace.

Kindness is God's graciousness working through me. It's having a sweet attitude mixed with sincerity in action. Doing kindness to others is following Jesus' example on the earth. There will always be a time to be kind to others as well as being instructive and a disciplinarian. Goodness means to give help and share in benevolence. It also means to help others grow in God's grace. It's like being a mentor or coach in life.

The last three elements involve my relationship with myself. Without faith, I cannot please God. Thank goodness that he provides the faith. I can trust Jesus Christ. I can be committed to any task he puts in front of me because he is reliable. When I have the top three elements in their proper place, I can grow in the last three and they will result in the middle three. Daily trust in his promises and watching them work will develop a sure faith.

A gentle spirit is one that is submissive. It is teachable and considerate. Self-control falls right into place as each characteristic is displayed.

God's grace is at work. His graciousness will be seen through the fruit.

The last element of the spiritual reality test is self-control. I cannot be master of myself through self-diligence. It is empowered through the Holy Spirit. It involves discipline, a deep drive and a determined sense of self-denial which is everything that goes against the nature of man. I have to remind myself that I am a new creation in Jesus Christ and that makes all the difference. I am challenged every day to celebrate life my magnifying Jesus Christ. When I face conflicts, I face them with Jesus Christ as my advocate. A celebrated life involves conflicts.

Dear Heavenly Father,

I pray that through conflicts I would respond in the way that would glorify you. I know interpersonal tension can cause many issues. Help me to be a peacemaker. Please help me to characterize the fruit of the Spirit. This is my desire in conflict.

I love you. Amen.

Personal Response

1. What has the chapter taught me? *(Overview)*

2. What level of commitment do I have in this study? *(Attitude)*

3. Who is my reliable resource? *(Confidence)*

4. What spiritual transformation have I learned? *(Discipleship)*

5. Have I experienced spiritual illumination? *(Enlightenment)*

6. What does the word "light" mean in this chapter? *(Understanding)*

7. Will I put the principal found in the chapter into prayer and practice it? *(Relationship)*

8. Will I share what I have learned in the chapter? *(Communication)*

CHAPTER EIGHT

Justice

JOHN 8:24

Life becomes a celebration as I learn to follow Jesus. If I refuse God, there are permanent consequences. Jesus said, "I told you that you would die in your sins; if you do not believe that I am the one I claim to be, you will indeed die in your sins." (John 8:24). A full and abundant life has become reality for me when I trusted in Jesus. (John 10:10). What a comparison! To magnify Christ's life is to live with the understanding that he is in me. Therefore, I have to keep in mind whatever hinders my intimacy with him must be dealt with. To die in sin is to die forever separated from being in a love relationship with God. According to Jesus, if we do not believe in him, we will not only die a physical death but a spiritual one as well. In the Bible, the second death is a spiritual one (Revelation 20:6,14). This will result in eternal separation from God. I do not like the word "hell" but this is what Jesus calls the place that all sinners will be separated to eternally.

Hell was not created for human occupation but rather for the fallen angels — angels who chose to go their own way instead of obeying their creator. (Matthew 25:41). All who reject God's will ultimately will be cast out of his presence and life forever in a conscious state of eternal separation from God in hell. Let's keep in mind that there is a choice. If we choose to reject him freely, we choose to live without him forever.

God does not force his love on me. He is persuasive but never coercive. He will respect my choice even when he knows the reality could be total separation. Hell has been established to punish evil. Since God is just, he must judge everyone who has sinned and broken his moral law. People who are unwilling to admit their guilt and ask for forgiveness are heading for justice. God's judgement is always right. Judgement will be according to my deeds (Romans 2:6; Revelation 20:12; Psalm 51:4b). The moral law is based on the nature of God. (Psalm 51:4a). When I sin, I am devaluing the image of God and I sin against God.

Sin is a willful violation of God's law. His solution to the problem of sin is Jesus Christ. Jesus Christ's blood on the cross has become my eternal shield to protect me from the wrath of a holy and awesome God. I have not refused God's generous offer of an eternal covering of my sin. Rejection is a personal choice. Sin cannot be ignored. It has to be confessed. I hate to say it but everyone who will go to hell has chosen to be there.

Sin is the problem and has caused the wrath of God to act. The divine remedy is found in Jesus Christ. The word 'salvation' means Savior (Acts 20:28). The word communicates the thought of deliverance, safety preservation, soundness, restoration and healing. Salvation provides a dismissal and removal of every charge against the sinner. It equips him with eternal life in place of death, with the perfect merit of Christ in place of condemnation. It provides forgiveness and justification in place of wrath. A celebrated life means justice.

Dear Heavenly Father,

Than you for saving me from your wrath and judgement for sin. I know I was born with a sinful nature. I am thankful for your justice. I rejoice in my deliverance. I pray for the people that are ignorant of this truth. I pray for people to take time to think about eternity.

I love you. Amen

Personal Response

1. What has the chapter taught me? *(Overview)*

2. What level of commitment do I have in this study? *(Attitude)*

3. Who is my reliable resource? *(Confidence)*

4. What spiritual transformation have I learned?
    (Discipleship)

5. Have I experienced spiritual illumination?
    (Enlightenment)

6. What does the word "light" mean in this chapter? *(Understanding)*

7. Will I put the principal found in the chapter into prayer and practice it? *(Relationship)*

8. Will I share what I have learned in the chapter? *(Communication)*

CHAPTER NINE

Blindness

JOHN 9:39-40

Life becomes a celebration as I learn to follow Jesus. Miracles have been performed to meet human needs. They also present a spiritual truth. They are existing because they have become Jesus' credentials. In his miracle with the blind man, he used it to be the basis for a short sermon on spiritual blindness. (John 9:39-41).

When I was a little boy, I fell down on the school playground and hurt my eye. One of my eyes came in contact with ice patches from the ground. It caused a period of unrest, worry and concern. I had to wear a bandage on the eye until it healed. At school, I seemed to be a hero; of course, I did make a touchdown playing football on all that ice. Some students were assigned to me to help me get around. Being in the dark is scary. Through God's help, I made it through the experience and can see alright. Spiritual darkness is a greater concern. The verse that stands out in this story for me in regard to blindness is "For judgement came I into the world that they that see not may see, and that they that see may become blind." (v.39). The miracle becomes a parable. A parable is a story or principle that conveys a meaning indirectly by the use of comparison. It's a "dark saying, a proverb."

The miracle illustrates the consequences of belief and unbelief. Persistent faith brought healing and progressive enlightenment. The unbelief of the Pharisees began with misunderstanding both of the law and of the person of Jesus. The law was for them a tradition to be kept and not a living voice. The result of this attitude was a prejudice that blinded the Pharisees to anything but their own preconceived opinions and so made them ignorant of the full truth. Pride prevented them from leaning any more and their bigotry caused them to drive Jesus away.

John 9:39 does not contradict 3:16-17. Jesus came for my salvation but the result of his coming was condemnation of those who would not believe. The religious leaders were blind and would not admit it. Therefore, the light of truth only made them more blind. Look around and you will see the people that are blind and do not want to see. As for them, they have knowledge. My heart goes out to them because they are really lost. Jesus calls those people "blind leaders of the blind." (Matthew 15:14). They have become blind through their pride, self-righteousness, traditions and false interpretation of the Word of God. Ignoring the evidence caused them to decide to follow their own will.

I have talked to several people that are spiritually blind. I am deeply concerned for them. Some think:

- That God is unknowable
- That God doesn't exist
- That it is not crucial to understand
- That they are the judge of human events
- That self and me-ism are the way
- That parts of the Bible are alright but deny other parts

- That the Bible is the Word of God but other books are equal to it
- That salvation must be obtained through good works
- That God is impersonal
- That it is foolish to think that there is only one way to God
- That there is no evil in the world
- That there are too many contradictions in the Bible
- That the Bible is not relevant

Jesus is the light of the world. (John 8:12; 9:5). The only people who cannot see the light are blind people and those who refuse to look and those who make themselves blind. "If any man wills to do God's will, he shall know of the doctrine." (John 7:17). I am glad that I am not blind. "The path of the just is as the shining light that shineth more and more unto the perfect day." (Proverbs 4:18). A celebrated life involves blotting out blindness and seeing through God's grace.

Dear Heavenly Father,

I am so grateful that you have opened my eyes to the truth. I pray for the blind to help them see the truth, to help pride, self-righteousness, traditions and false interpretations of the Word of God not to get in the way. My heart goes out to the lost. Help me be a light to them.

I love you. Amen

Personal Response

1. What has the chapter taught me? *(Overview)*

2. What level of commitment do I have in this study? *(Attitude)*

3. Who is my reliable resource? *(Confidence)*

4. What spiritual transformation have I learned? *(Discipleship)*

5. Have I experienced spiritual illumination? *(Enlightenment)*

6. What does the word "light" mean in this chapter? *(Understanding)*

7. Will I put the principal found in the chapter into prayer and practice it? *(Relationship)*

8. Will I share what I have learned in the chapter? *(Communication)*

CHAPTER TEN

Abundance

JOHN 10:9-11

L ife becomes a celebration as I learn to follow Jesus. I can enjoy an abundant life in the Lord. I have the assurance of a full and free life. Jesus not only gave his life for me but he has given his life to me right now. Jesus has delivered me from bondage. I have salvation in him. The word "saved" means delivered safe and sound. I can rest on what he says because of what he has done. He died for me. (John 10:11-13). Five times in this sermon, Jesus clearly affirmed the sacrificial nature of his death. He died as a substitute willingly laying down his life for me. His dying is efficient only for those who will believe. He also knows me. Knowing means intimate relationship, not intellectual awareness. He knows my name (v. 3) and knows my nature and needs. (Psalm 23:1,6). He takes up his life again (v. 17-18). His voluntary death was followed by his victorious resurrection. He yielded up his spirit to the Father and he voluntarily took up his life again and arose from the dead. The Father gave him the authority in love. If I don't believe, I will die in my sins. I am able to live life to the fullest because of what Jesus has done for me.

An abundant lifestyle involves living with the resurrection power. I have made the decision to follow the Lord wholeheartedly. I have had to learn to organize my life around the promise of God. I am not to hold anything back. I am to live by the absolutes of the Scripture and choose to keep to my convictions. I am to accept challenges and work my way through them. I am to live with unlimited faith that God has provided.

An abundant lifestyle involves gratitude. I have to develop a heart of appreciation. My conversation needs to be positive. Any negatives should push me forward into a deeper trust. When I get up in the morning, I have to discipline my mind to be thankful. God is gracious and there is always something to be grateful for. The positive list is always longer than the negative. I am thankful for opportunities, health, my children, grandchildren, friends, etc.

An abundant lifestyle involves praising others for their achievements. Encouragement is the center focus. Reflection on past accomplishments is replaced with helping the younger generation to become successful. One must have a peaceful acceptance of the reality of life and the adventure of new things around the corner and commitment to glorify the Lord Jesus Christ which helps in the adjustments of life.

An abundant lifestyle involves keeping the mind alert and grasping new ideas. There is no idea of stopping the thinking process. The goal setting and tackling of new ideas are always present. Change is not an enemy but a friend, reading and pursuing new disciplines, keeping current with events of the day and sharing interests with others keeps me moving ahead.

An abundant lifestyle involves seeing the big picture. Reading the daily headlines does not disturb me. I know who is in charge. My energy is flowing through the blood of Jesus. My life is not crippled with today's blindness and depression. There is a sense of confidence because God has the blueprint for life. The celebrated life involves abundance.

Dear Heavenly Father,
I pray that my lifestyle will present the truth of the abundant life. I experience life to the fullest because of the resurrection power. Help me to live out what it means to live in Christ. Thank you for your strength and presence.
I love you. Amen.

Personal Response

1. What has the chapter taught me? *(Overview)*

2. What level of commitment do I have in this study? *(Attitude)*

3. Who is my reliable resource? *(Confidence)*

4. What spiritual transformation have I learned? *(Discipleship)*

5. Have I experienced spiritual illumination? *(Enlightenment)*

6. What does the word "light" mean in this chapter? *(Understanding)*

7. Will I put the principal found in the chapter into prayer and practice it? *(Relationship)*

8. Will I share what I have learned in the chapter? *(Communication)*

CHAPTER ELEVEN

Emotions

JOHN 11:35

Life becomes a celebration as I learn to follow Jesus. In my childhood, I learned the shortest verse in the Bible, "Jesus wept." (John 11:35). I heard the story about a family that had experienced sickness and then death. I discovered the emotions involved in the story. Emotion is a psychological state that arises spontaneously. It is often accompanied by physiological change which is a feeling of sadness, anger, joy, sorrow, reverence, hate and love.

Our feelings are important. We cannot neglect their influence on our lives. Feelings are neither right nor wrong and they are simply there. What I do with a feeling makes it right or wrong. Feelings are vital and necessary in our makeup as human beings. I have to understand them. Denial will result in emotional illness.

I have had to learn to not trust my senses or my feelings. I don't live on whether it feels good or if it seems right. God has given us his Word to give guidance. I am not led by what is right in my own eyes. I have to exercise faith in God's Word and not in human reason regardless of the false signals sent out by my senses. Life requires many adjustments in the different transitions that have to be made in life. Following my senses is a gradual process and will result in a habitual choice pattern. A continued reliance on God is necessary to keep me in a straight and level position headed in God's direction.

I don't remember who said this but it is a good statement: "You do what you do and you feel what you feel because you think what you think." The mind accounts for your ability to think, remember, love hate, feel reason, imagine and analyze. The body also responds physically to its direction. The Bible says that I should control my mind. "Guard your heart" (Proverbs 4:23), "take captive every thought (2 Corinthians 10:5), "temptation begins in my mind" (James 1:13). Believe it or not, that mind can be controlled but it takes discipline and hard work (Hebrews 12:11).

The next three thoughts come from my book entitled, "Thoughts To Ponder" published through Torch Publishing Company in 1984. Controlling the mind and my feelings involves the renewed mind. The Bible says, "And be not conformed to this world; but be ye transformed by the renewing of our mind, that ye may prove what is that good and acceptable and perfect will of God." (Romans 12:2). Our minds need to be re-educated. Whatever we have learned we can also unlearn, relearn or change through the re-education process. It is a wonderful thing to look at the world objectively, yet with hope, faith and love. "Christian Re-educative Self-Counseling" will help us to become more sensitive and alert to our fallibilities, as well as to our potentialities and will help us to become less mechanistic and less fatalistic.

We must accept responsibility for our thinking, feelings and behavior. We reject the theory that we are wholly determined by our past. Our mental lives need to be based on reason and our spiritual lives need to be based on faith. We are dealing with an objective analysis of your perceptions, thinking, feeling and behavior. It is studying the facts and events (our perceptions) and our emotive feelings. Get the facts, be objective and choose the feeling you really want to experience. The Bible says, "for as he thinketh in his heart, so is he." (Proverbs 23:7).

Controlling the mind and my feelings involves taking charge. The Bible says, "we are troubled on every side yet not distressed." (2 Corinthians 4:8). In reading this text, we can discover for ourselves that a tremendous choice over our feelings and learning to look above and beyond ourselves is possible. God says take charge of your life through the Holy Spirit's guidance.

The basic problem that most people experience is that they operate more on feelings than on reason. They would rather rely on their sense organs than their mind. Everything that goes into the mind must be evaluated with objective thinking. Our minds are filled with memories, rational and irrational belief, ideas, attitudes, prejudices, biases and fantasies. We are prone to misinterpret, misjudge and misunderstand; therefore, we suffer.

The Bible says, "Beloved, believe not every spirit, but try the spirits whether they are of God . . . every spirit that confesseth that Jesus Christ is come in the flesh is of God." (1 John 4:1,2). We must feed our minds with the right kind of food. Eating garbage will produce unhealthy results; confusion, doubts, fears, jealousy, anger and hostility. Let us recognize what is wrong and why and become firmly committed to change. Let us take charge of our lives by allowing God to work in us.

Controlling the mind and my feelings involves being obedient. The Bible says, "For the weapons of our warfare are not carnal, but mighty through God to the pulling down of strongholds, casting down imaginations and every high thing that exalteth itself against the knowledge of God, and bringing into captivity every thought to the obedience of Christ." (2 Corinthians 10:4,5). This obedience is possible because of what Christ has already done. Because of Christ's victory on the cross, we have a right to evict the thoughts that come from the flesh and the devil.

We must refocus our thought life, not to win the victory, but to receive the victory that has already been won. Only if we understand our authority can our minds be renewed. Receiving Christ as Savior gives us a new nature, but the old thought patterns often continue. In Jesus Christ's name is our authority — let's take charge through him. We must reprogram our minds with God's Word and his Word will increase our faith. Our lives would be changed if we spent twenty minutes with God each day before 9:00 AM. It would keep us spiritually refreshed and we would begin each day committing ourselves to God.

The Bible says, "Watch over your heart with all diligence, for from it flow the springs of life." (Proverbs 4:23). We must fill our minds with the wonder of Christ and desire to be like him. We must have verses of Scripture ready to quote at a moment's notice. We must always be ready to combat lies with the truth of God's Word. God himself must be first in our thinking. Do you want to master yourself just so you can have a clear conscience, live a successful life and raise a fine family? Or are you fully committed to living the praise of God's glory?

God lets us struggle so that in the end we will have a greater appreciation of him. Don't run from him when you fail, but run to him. He's waiting for us to give up our toys and fully surrender our hearts to him. What kind of relationship do we have with God? Controlling the mind and my feelings involves being a doer. The Bible says, "But be ye doers of the word, and not hearers only, deceiving your own selves." (James 1:22). Millions of people are needlessly suffering from a wide range of serious afflictions, difficulties and problems, including physical and emotional disorders which are often self-induced and self-maintained. Perhaps as much as 70% of our physical and emotional problems are caused by ourselves.

"All is well" in our churches, communities and country, is not at all the truth. Many leaders are fearfully afraid to stick their necks out, to be disliked, to rock the boat, to upset the status quo, or to lose the support (financial and otherwise) of their followers. Unless people begin to grasp the reality of their lives and begin to appreciate the condition of the world and the task God has set before us, there will be little hope for the future.

The problems are remaining because we have made Jesus Christ fit our thinking, our ideologies, our dogmas, our churches, our customs, our folkways and we are trying to interpret him from our own so very limited knowledge and experience while rejecting the very foundation of his teaching. We have failed to listen to Jesus Christ who tells us to pray and work, to have faith and reason, to hear and do and to follow his footsteps. The Bible says, "Be a doer of the Word." A celebrated life involves my emotions.

Dear Heavenly Father,
I pray that I will always do the right things when it comes to feelings. Thank you for your word to give direction. Help me to continue in my reliance upon you. Thank you for giving me emotions and sensitivity. Help me be a doer of the word.
I love you. Amen.

Personal Response

1. What has the chapter taught me? *(Overview)*

2. What level of commitment do I have in this study? *(Attitude)*

3. Who is my reliable resource? *(Confidence)*

4. What spiritual transformation have I learned? *(Discipleship)*

5. Have I experienced spiritual illumination? *(Enlightenment)*

6. What does the word "light" mean in this chapter? *(Understanding)*

7. Will I put the principal found in the chapter into prayer and practice it? *(Relationship)*

8. Will I share what I have learned in the chapter? *(Communication)*

Praise

JOHN 12:12-16

L ife becomes a celebration as I learn to follow Jesus. As I come to Chapter Twelve of the Gospel of John, I am always excited about the "triumphal entry of Jesus into Jerusalem." It is one of the few incidents in Jesus' life reported in all four Gospels. By this action, he presented himself officially to the nation as the Messiah and Son of God. Jesus entered the city on his own time and forced the whole issue in order that it might happen exactly on the Passover day when the lambs were being sacrificed. The Bible says, "Christ our Passover was sacrificed for us." (1 Corinthians 5:7, 1 Peter 1:19). In God's perfect timing, he presented himself to die.

The word "Hosanna" found in this passage means "give salvation now." It was a term of praise. I would have liked to be there waving a palm branch. I believe that he is the Son of God and the Son of Man. He is the supernatural one — deity — and is a human being and my substitute. I want to give him adoration, admiration and acclamation.

Singing Hallelujah . . . praising the Lord should be a natural part of life. Hallelujah, he has brought himself into my presence. I have a promised helper. It is hard to believe that he indwells in me. He is only a breath away. I am learning to breathe out my impurities and breathe in his presence.

Hallelujah, he has brought happiness. In being sensitive to sin and following his initiative, my roots are becoming grounded. Seeking his kingdom brings joy. Learning to live in his presence brings security. Hallelujah, he has brought victory even when surrounded with helplessness. Learning and coping skills are available in Jesus Christ. "It is he that hath made us and we are his." (Psalm 100:3). He created me and I belong ti him. Making the adjustment to abide in him is the key.

Hallelujah, he has brought comfort during the time that disease entered my death-doomed body. Keep in mind there is the promise of the redemption of the body for which all true believers wait. God has said until then, "I am with you, I will watch over you and I will give you rest." (Genesis 18:15; Matthew 11:28). Those words bring comfort and strength in illness. As I recite his word (Matthew 6, Psalm 23) and reflect on his past answered promises, I can rely on having right-thinking during suffering.

Hallelujah, he has brought hope. I hope my praisecanbecontagiousandbringencouragement, exhortation and confident expectation. I am learning to trust in Jesus. He is worth believing. My hope is built on Jesus' name. I regularly recite his names. "He is called wonderful, counselor, the mighty God, everlasting Father and the Prince of Peace." (Isaiah 9:6). I review his names in my mind and I rehearse their meaning. Then, I act upon them by being amazed with his wonder and reading his Word to obtain wisdom. He is the mighty God and everlasting Father which gives me confidence because he is sovereign. Peace will be the goal and ultimate reality of praise.

There are many ways to praise the Lord. I praise him when I find pleasure in him. I praise him when I worship him. I praise him when I share his faithfulness. I praise him when I model a Christ-like life. I praise him when I find delight in his Word. I praise him when I get up in the morning and say good morning to him and when I end the day asking him if he had good company with me. I praise him when I say 'I love you for who you are, not just for what you have blessed me with.' I praise him when I study and share his Word.

I have used Psalm 150 hundreds of times to introduce my trumpet solos or ensemble performances. I have preached from the text and have taught it in the classroom. I have been reminded of it when I listen to great symphonies. In only six verses, it emphasizes thirteen times to praise the Lord. Each word like each note in an overture is very important. When I put it all together, it will show God's majesty, excellence and greatness.

The word 'praise,' or 'hallelujah,' means to honor, respect and admire. It is a shout of joy, reverence and gratitude. The word 'Lord' in the Hebrew language means ownership. He is in absolute control. He is the governor of the whole earth and beyond. I have the privilege to praise the supreme one because the 'ye' refers to me. The words 'praise God' clarified the fullness of his divine power. His name 'Yahweh' is defined as he is the self-existent one, the supreme personal intelligence, the creator and preserver of all things. The divine trinity is worthy of singing Hallelujah to. He is tripersonal and has the same nature. What a history to behold! God the Father is the creator God — God the Son is the redeemer God and God the Spirit is the sustainer God.

"Praise ye the Lord . . . praise God in his sanctuary." Just think of it: I am his sanctuary. The church is his dwelling place and I am a part of that body. What a tremendous responsibility and awesome opportunity to praise . . . pause for a moment and then say 'thank you' to God on your knees.

"Praise him in the firmament of his power." He is not only here and present with us but now he expands his territory to everywhere. Look around, look into the depths of the sea and look up into the heavens. What splendor, what glory, what radiance and what unapproachable light. When I look at the earth from the firmament, I realize the earth spins on its axis. It doesn't spin too fast lest I be thrown off. It doesn't spin too slow lest I feel it and become dizzy to death. It spins just right so I neither fall nor feel dizzy because it spins at the same rate as my ability to function within the force of gravity. I have an awesome God.

Praise him for his mighty acts. God is totally responsible for all creation. His sovereignty concerns his absolute rule and control. It is beyond me to understand but through faith I accept. Think of it, he knows all things, he is all powerful, he is everywhere present and we have the duty and right to bow before him in praise and say in humility 'hallelujah.' But he doesn't stop there and he goes further. He says, "praise him according to his excellent greatness." I am on my knees as I reflect on his holiness. As I think of all his knowledge and that he knows how to use it (wisdom), I thank him for my blessings and realize I can count them because of his goodness. His excellent greatness is seen in his grace. I don't deserve it but I have experienced his unmerited favor.

Now I have come to his orchestration — a symphony of praise and a Hallelujah Chorus. The sound of the trumpet reveals the wind instrument that will get my attention. They blast the heralders' notes of praise. The psaltery and harp reveal the string instruments that bring unity and harmony. The timbrel, cymbals, organ pipes and dance will reveal the percussion instruments that will unite all the instruments into a complete voice of praise.

"Let everything that hath breath praise the Lord." God breathed everything into existence. He is the giver of life. He provides the breath to praise. There is no other direction to follow. Every breath I take is given through God's grace. He has given life to the fullest. Every moment of every day I take in air to breathe to sustain life. This should be a reminder to praise him.

Therefore, it is a natural part of life to "shout Hallelujah." A celebrated life involves praise.

Dear Heavenly Father,

I pray that you will accept my praise. The longer I live, the longer I want to praise you. I praise you because you are the supernatural one — deity — and you have taken on human nature to be my substitute and are now interceding for me.

I love you. Amen.

Personal Response

1. What has the chapter taught me? *(Overview)*

2. What level of commitment do I have in this study? *(Attitude)*

3. Who is my reliable resource? *(Confidence)*

4. What spiritual transformation have I learned? *(Discipleship)*

5. Have I experienced spiritual illumination? *(Enlightenment)*

6. What does the word "light" mean in this chapter? *(Understanding)*

7. Will I put the principal found in the chapter into prayer and practice it? *(Relationship)*

8. Will I share what I have learned in the chapter? *(Communication)*

CHAPTER THIRTEEN

Love

Life becomes a celebration as I learn to follow Jesus. He said, "Love one another, even as I have loved you" (John 13:34). Love is a permanent badge of discipleship and a foundation of unity. What is involved with his kind of love? I think I have to look at his love for his disciples. He said, "I have loved them unto the end" (John 13:1). What was his last demonstration of love? This love is a preview of the meaning of the cross.

His love was freely given. It couldn't be quenched with evil in spite of his full knowledge of the coming betrayal and denial. I have to demonstrate love even if good people don't understand my determination to serve and be dedicated to Jesus, or if bad people criticize, ridicule, harass and gossip.

His love was given with a submissiveness. Jesus was aware of his exalted powers. He deliberately subjected himself to the needs of his disciples. I am not a victim to the enemy. I have voluntarily given my will to love. My time, energy and gifts are his. He has enabled me.

His love transcended the barriers of social class. He was conscious of his divine origin and of his divine destiny. I am also determined to cross over any class distinction. When my own inadequacies come into the picture, I have to realize who I am representing. I am honored to serve all nationalities, all income brackets, all intellectual levels and all spiritual levels of maturity.

His love is active. Twice it is stated that the supper was interrupted. Jesus took the responsibility to prepare the disciples to eat. Washing their feet was the task. Whatever the task, washing the toilets in the bathroom or dusting the pulpit, I must be willing to take the initiative. Whatever my gifts are, he will provide opportunity to enrich his kingdom.

His love cleansing must be constant. A thorough washing or cleansing took place on the cross through Jesus Christ's blood. This cleansing is a once-for-all task. The co0nstant cleansing is to remove daily encounters with sin. Every day will bring a time to bow before the Master and to be convicted of sin and to confess.

I want to infect others with the love of Jesus. I know God loves me because the Bible tells me so, but do I really experience his love for me? When I became a father, I discovered what my heavenly Father's love was like even in a mot limited way. My nature is to show love by touch, word, time and excitement. I am here and I am listening and I have time for you. My love is not built on fear or guilt. Jesus said, "Love the Lord your God with all your heart, with all your soul and with all your mind" (Matthew 22:37-38). When was the last time I simply hugged the Lord?

Sometimes I think I am alone. No one really understands me. Then God's Word reminds me that he knew me before he made me (Jeremiah 1:4,5). He is not only sovereign but he intimately knows me. As I digest this truth, it has changed my daily perspective in life. It is an astonishing fact, God treasures me. The Holy Creator sees me as his glorious inheritance (Ephesians 1:18). He anticipates my departure from the earth to be with him. I call him Abba Father.

To experience true love (Jesus' example), I have to spend time pursuing it. My prayer "earnestly I seek him, I thirst for him, my body longs for him" (Psalm 63:1-5). I am driven with a person within. To experience true love, I have to let Jesus in (Revelation 3:20). I do not have to try harder and I do not have to feed my inadequacies. I do not need to be driven by guilt.

I hold to the truth "Come near to God and he will come near to you" (James 4:8). I have memorized its words and meaning. It has given support and encouragement. It has given peace and joy and given a spirit of triumph. It has provided love.

To experience true love, I need God to help me love God. The supernatural has to take place. Genuine love is produced through the indwelling of the Holy Spirit. To experience true love, I must start running toward it. My constant focus on Jesus will keep me from sin. Freedom from past guilt, injustice, worry, analyzing and road blocks will be removed. To experience true love, I have to expect trouble (John 16:33), but I also anticipate overcoming. A celebrated life involves true love.

Dear Heavenly Father,

I am thankful for your love. Help me to continue to love you. I know genuine love is produced through the indwelling of the Holy Ghost. I want my constant focus to be on you. I expect trouble in my life but I also expect to overcome.

I love you. Amen.

Personal Response

1. What has the chapter taught me? *(Overview)*

2. What level of commitment do I have in this study? *(Attitude)*

3. Who is my reliable resource? *(Confidence)*

4. What spiritual transformation have I learned? *(Discipleship)*

5. Have I experienced spiritual illumination? *(Enlightenment)*

6. What does the word "light" mean in this chapter? *(Understanding)*

7. Will I put the principal found in the chapter into prayer and practice it? *(Relationship)*

8. Will I share what I have learned in the chapter? *(Communication)*

CHAPTER FOURTEEN

Comfort

JOHN 14:1-6

Life becomes a celebration as I learn to follow Jesus. The promise of comfort is provided by Jesus Christ, not only in his future return but also in the present with the ministry of the Holy Spirit (v.26). The scene is in the Upper Room where the disciples had gathered. The work of the disciples was about to be shattered. Confusion, bewilderment, anxiety and devastation would transpire. The word "troubled" involves many words to describe their hopelessness. Jesus thinks back to his words, "my soul is troubled" which describe his deep horror facing the wrath of God on our behalf.

Jesus' departure would be for their advantage since he was going to prepare a heavenly home for them and would return to take them so that they might be with him. This passage refers to taking believers from earth to live in heaven. I am grateful that his words, "I am the way, truth and life" have brought confidence to my life. As I reflect on the past few chapters of the Gospel of John, I have been given comfort to face tomorrow.

A celebrated life involves communication. Jesus communicated God to humanity. He is the "word." The word is a means to communicate God to mankind. The indwelling of God is accomplished through Jesus. I pray that I might be a good communicator of the faith.

A celebrated life involves relationships. New relationships bring freshness to life. A relationship with Jesus brings intimacy with God. Building relationships is important. I pray that I might learn to follow Christ's model in making relationships.

A celebrated life involves sufficiency. The Scripture says, "My grace is sufficient." I can rely upon his word. Sufficiency is a sure thing because God is sovereign. He is in charge. I pray that I will learn to be dependent upon Jesus alone.

A celebrated life involves transformation. Transformation takes place when I fully accept Jesus' claims and commands. An internal change of a person's nature through God's grace takes place when I believe in Jesus. Faith is the process for Jesus to enter the heart. I pray that I can model the transformation that has taken place in my life.

A celebrated life involves worship. This depends on my heart relationship with God. Worship involves truth and the spirit. Worship requires love, the whole person, my spirit and time. I pray that I can be God-conscious at all times. I have to learn to practice his presence.

A celebrated life involves belief. Believing involves faith. When I believe in Jesus, I received the gift of faith. Faith requires complete submission and aggressive trust. It is easy for me to trust Jesus because he is God. He is real and genuine. I pray that I can be confident in my reliance on him.

A celebrated life involves selection. Saving faith is a gift of God. It is an act of the will and mind. It is a spiritual union brought about by God himself. He has chosen me. I have responded to that call. I pray that thanksgiving will always be in my heart. I do not merit his grace.

A celebrated life involves conflict. Interpersonal tension surrounds everyday living. Jesus was a peacemaker. Transformation within brings change outwardly in my behavior. Resolving conflict involves determination, effort and skill. It demands desire, constant development and application. I pray that I will yield my will to Jesus and thus I will think biblically.

A celebrated life involves justice. Consequences of evil behavior will certainly become a part of my life. God loves me and will discipline me because he loves me. Whatever hinders my intimacy with Jesus must be dealt with. I pray that I will choose to live for him and will please him in all my activities.

A celebrated life involves blindness. I am speaking of understanding spiritual blindness. The parable is about a blind man that is able to see through Jesus performing a miracle. The miracle illustrates the consequences of belief and unbelief. The Pharisees were blinded by their own preconceived opinions and therefor ignorant of the full truth. Christ's coming brought salvation and condemnation. I am thankful that I am not blind and pray that I will be a bright light shining in a world that is blind.

A celebrated life involves abundance. Jesus not only gave his life for me, but he has given his life to me right now. I live a full and complete life in him. I am learning to organize my life around his promises. The key is a wholehearted attitude of submission. I pray that every day energy will be in my bloodstream because of his blood that was shed for me.

A celebrated life involves emotions. Feelings are important. They are neither right or wrong. What I do with a feeling makes it right or wrong. Life is made up of many transitions. A continued reliance upon God is necessary to keep in a straight-level position. This will lead toward God's direction. Feelings have to be directed through the "renewed mind." I pray that my spirit will lead the way of my soul and my soul will lead the way of my body and that all of me will be yielded to the Holy Spirit.

A celebrated life involves praise. Praising Jesus Christ is a natural part of life. I want to give personal adoration to him. I want to give public admiration to him. I want to acclaim Jesus with enthusiasm to everyone that I come in contact with. I pray that happiness, comfort, sensitivity to sin, hope and reverent gratitude will be found in my shout for joy.

A celebrated life involves love. God loves me and treasures me. The holy creator sees me as his glorious inheritance (Ephesians 1:18). He anticipates my departure from the earth to be with him. I call him "Abba Father." I pray that the Holy Spirit will produce genuine love in me for him and the creation that he has made.

A celebrated life involves comfort. When my heart is troubled, I only have to review the previous chapters and I will be filled with comfort. I do not live with hopelessness because my hope is in Jesus Christ. I live with eternity and heaven in mind. My testing is found in Jesus who said, "let not your heart be troubled." This is my prayer. A celebrated life involves comfort.

Dear Heavenly Father,

Thank you that through suffering I can have your comfort. I have only to remember your promises. As I draw near to you, you will draw near to me. I am resting in you.

I love you. Amen.

Personal Response

1. What has the chapter taught me? *(Overview)*

2. What level of commitment do I have in this study? *(Attitude)*

3. Who is my reliable resource? *(Confidence)*

4. What spiritual transformation have I learned? *(Discipleship)*

5. Have I experienced spiritual illumination? *(Enlightenment)*

6. What does the word "light" mean in this chapter? *(Understanding)*

7. Will I put the principal found in the chapter into prayer and practice it? *(Relationship)*

8. Will I share what I have learned in the chapter? *(Communication)*

CHAPTER FIFTEEN

Remain

JOHN 15: 4-5

Life becomes a celebration as I learn to follow Jesus. The Bible says, "Remain in me and I will remain in you." (John 13:4). The secret of producing fruit is remaining in the vine. To remain in Jesus means that his words remain in me (v.7). Loving Jesus will energize obedience to his commands (v.9-10). Joy will become a real part of my life and a sense of completeness will follow (v.11-12). There is confidence that comes with remaining in him because he has chosen me to bear fruit. Love for him and others will be the manifesting factor (v.17). Remaining in Jesus takes dedication to a developmental process. It moves me from the finite to the infinite while still in a mortal body.

Remaining begins with evaluating my spiritual condition. Limitless building can take place if I am sure of my salvation in Jesus. The Scripture says, "Examine yourselves to see whether you are in the faith; test yourselves." (1 Corinthians 13:5). Am I a new creation in Christ? Has anything changed in my life? How can I be certain I am justified? I can have assurance simply because God can be trusted. I have the testimony through his Word (1 John 5:9,12). God says that if I believe on Jesus as my Savior that I am justified. I have had to accept human testimony. Why shouldn't I accept God's testimony?

I also have an internal assurance. Do I see things differently? The Holy Spirit brings new understanding and views to divine truth. The soul can discern the truth of God. To confess that Jesus is the Christ is to confess the Christ of the Scriptures. The teaching of the Holy Spirit in one's life brings assurance of faith. I have discovered that as I search the Scriptures, it leads to a righteous life. It doesn't mean that I will be sinless. It means an increased dissatisfaction with sin. I am in Jesus Christ because I am desirous to keep his Word. A genuine love causes me to remain and abide in him. Morally, I seek to follow Jesus and be an example to others. As I yield wholeheartedly to the Holy Spirit, he produces the character that is needed. Love is the mark by which the world may know the true Christians. Regeneration will produce love. Love is an attitude which determines what I do.

Remaining continues with participation. To be a follower of Jesus Christ means action, not observation. I need to present my spirit, soul and body to Jesus. It has to take place in that order. The spirit dictates to the soul what to do and the soul tells the body how to respond. The inner man is the spirit. It is the breath of God. It is that part of me that is united to the Holy Spirit. God's Word becomes a part of the inner being, the spirit. By using the Scripture, spending time in it, memorizing it and meditating on it, it will develop my spirit to become spiritual. The world wants to control the mind but God wants to transform it. The mind is a part of the soul and will change from within. The Holy Spirit changes my mind by releasing power from within. The inner man (spirit) will tell the mind (soul) what to think. The will is united to the mind and tells it what to do. The body is the dwelling place of the Holy Spirit and must be surrendered to the Lord. Yielding body, soul and spirit to the Holy Spirit will keep me abiding in Jesus.

Remaining includes a thorough working knowledge of the Bible. Filling the heart with knowledge without the heart will leave only emptiness. Learning to handle the word of truth correctly is necessary (2 Timothy 2:15). This takes discipline, dedication and discernment. The psalmist shared this reference from the Scripture. "Thy word is very pure, therefore thy servant loves it . . . the sum of thy word is truth and every one of the righteous ordinances is everlasting." (Psalm 119: 140,160). I must believe in its authority. The Bible says, "And he reasoned in the synagogue . . . and persuaded the Jews and Greeks . . . and he continued . . . teaching the Word of God among them." (Acts 18:4,11). I know of no other way to give the authority of the Scriptures than to continue teaching the Word. I would like to reason and persuade you but the Scripture is a living, vital agency with supernatural power in itself. Read the promise, "For as the rain cometh down and the snow from heaven, and returneth not thither, but watereth the earth, and maketh it bring forth and bud, that it may give seed to the sower, and bread to the eater; so shall my Word be that goeth forth out of my mouth; it shall not return unto me void, but it shall accomplish that which I please, and it shall prosper in the thing whereto I send it." (Isaiah 55:10,11). To the same purpose Jeremiah has written: "Is not my word like as a fire? Saith the Lord; and like a hammer that breaketh the rock in pieces?" (Jeremiah 23:29). God uses his Word "For the Word of God is quick (living) and powerful (active) and sharper than any two-edged sword, piercing even to the dividing asunder of soul and spirit, and of the joints and marrow, and is discerned of the thoughts and intents (ideas) of the heart." (Hebrews 4:12).

The Bible is an ancient book for modern times. It is one book, one history, one story and one mind produced it. God himself became a man so that we might know what to think of when we think of God. (John 1:14; 14:9). I could give all the evidence for scriptural authority but why don't you read the Bible for yourself and let it prove itself?

I must apply it to my life. The Bible says, "As newborn babes, desire the sincere milk of the word that ye may grow thereby." (1 Peter 2:2). God has given his Word so that believers may grow thereby. We haven't fulfilled our obligations to the Word until application has taken place. The Bible is not only the source book for today. Growth in the spiritual life comes not merely from hearing but from hearing and doing. The Bible says, "the effectual doer shall be blesses in what he does." (James 1:25). If you know these things, you are blessed if you do them.

The Bible has been given so that man's basic nature can be changed. "All Scripture is given by God and is profitable for teaching, for reproof, for correction, for training in righteousness, that the man of God may be adequate, equipped for every good work." (2 Timothy 3:16,17). It teaches, rebukes, restores and trains for righteous living. It equips us to the work that God wants us to do. The Bible convicts, regenerates, nurtures, cleanses, counsels, guides, prevents sin, revives, strengthens, gives wisdom, delivers and helps. The Bible alone realistically and sufficiently meets man's deepest problems, longings, needs and inadequacies. It provides the answer to man's needs for deliverance from the penalty of sin, for spiritual progress, daily victory, for guidance and personal relationships and conduct. As we learn the Scriptures, let us apply it to our daily activities.

I must study it as a life source. The Bible says, "Blessed are the undefiled in the way, who walk in the law of the Lord." (Psalm 119:1). What is wrong with reading the Bible? Why do people think it so strange? Some people have the idea that the Bible is just for the mentally weak, some people think it is for the ignorant, some people imagine that is just for the shut-ins and some think it is only for the children. Why do teens and young adults turn from it? I believe they do not go on to read it, believe it, study it or follow it. If we are going to walk in the law of the Lord, we must follow this pattern.

First we need to study it through . . . that is . . . master a verse every day. Think of it . . . at the end of the year, you will have 365 verses in your heart and in your mind to bring about happiness, direction, peace and contentment. We need to pray about it. We must let each verse become a part of our very being, praying the verse right into reality, and then seeing the promises of God change our lives as we claim them. We must write down our thoughts. We cannot remember everything but our computer mind has it and we need to refresh our memory. That, of course, brings us to working it out. Let the Bible get in your heart, pray about it, work it out and then live it. We must also pass it on. We must talk about it. Let the Word of God inspire and bless your heart. It takes discipline. You cannot be lazy. Walk in the law of the Lord and you will find purpose and peace. A celebrated life involves remaining in Christ.

Dear Heavenly Father,

Thank you for giving me the way and means to remain in you. I know I will not lose my passport to heaven when I make mistakes and sin. I realize that confessing is a daily discipline. I am just thankful that you have placed in my heart a passion for you. Thank you for your "Word." Help me to keep believing its authority. Help me to study and apply to all my activities.

I love you. Amen.

Personal Response

1. What has the chapter taught me? *(Overview)*

2. What level of commitment do I have in this study? *(Attitude)*

3. Who is my reliable resource? *(Confidence)*

4. What spiritual transformation have I learned? *(Discipleship)*

5. Have I experienced spiritual illumination? *(Enlightenment)*

6. What does the word "light" mean in this chapter? *(Understanding)*

7. Will I put the principal found in the chapter into prayer and practice it? *(Relationship)*

8. Will I share what I have learned in the chapter? *(Communication)*

CHAPTER SIXTEEN

Prayer

JOHN 16:24

Life becomes a celebration as I learn to follow Jesus. When I was a teenager, I memorized John 16:24, "until now you have not asked for anything in my name; ask and you will receive,and your joy will be complete." I was very interested in doing God's will. I have always had joy when I had fellowship with him. I anted to ask and receive. Jesus Christ prepares his disciples for the hatred that will be directed toward them. Persecution is going to be a part of their life. Jesus is going away and he wants to get them ready. The Holy Spirit is going to come and this will bring triumph and not tragedy. The work of the Holy Spirit is to convict or convince. He will convict of sin, righteousness, and of judgement. They were taught that the Holy Spirit would guide them into a complete knowledge of all truth. His main purpose would be to glorify Christ. Christ's pain and death and resurrection, joy and indwelling of the Spirit and return of Jesus Christ would produce permanent joy. Because of the finished work of Christ, I am able to come to the Father in Christ's name and be heard and responded to. The testimony of Jesus Christ is found in his eternity, his humiliation and his exaltation (v.28). I may experience tribulation in the world but will overcome because I have peace, joy and the privilege to love God the Father through Jesus Christ and the guidance of the Holy Spirit in prayer.

I have learned that if I want something from God I need to just pray. The process has been slow but steady. A condition of getting things is asking for them. After memorizing John 16:24, my mind and heart were turned to Matthew 7:7,8. This would start me on the path in praying in his name. This text says, "Ask, and it shall be given you; for everyone that asketh, receiveth; and he that seeketh findeth; and to him that knocketh it shall be opened." Jesus means exactly what he said. He says literally to keep on asking, keep seeking and keep knocking. He is eager to answer my prayers.

To pray in his name involves praying in faith. I have to ask in faith with confidence that I am responding to the Scripture in the correct way (Matthew 9:29). Keep in mind that faith is made up of two parts which are belief and unbelief. Remember the father who came to Jesus and said, "Lord, I believe; help thou mine unbelief." (Mark 9:24). His prayer was answered and his boy was healed. Faith can be found between unbelief and certainty. Asking fulfills the requirement of faith. Accept the faith that God has given and grow. As I claim his promises, I will grow. Asking is proof of faith.

To pray in his name involves his will (1 John 5:14,15). I have to know him. Learn to be submissive to the leading of the Holy Spirit. I am so thankful that the Spirit is my teacher. He is able to give understanding. An honest examination of the Word of God, understanding motives, listening to the Spirit and developing relationships are means to knowing his will. I am not alone — I have a helper (Romans 8:26). The Holy Spirit makes intercession for me. I must simply ask, be sincerer and honest and he will correct my prayers.

To pray in his name doesn't mean that I simply use that phrase at the end of my prayer. It means that what I ask for will please and give honor to the Lord Jesus. Ask things for Jesus' sake. I have to learn to ask for things that Jesus wants. I cannot do that if I do not spend time with him. I believe praying brings me into God's presence. The more I am in his presence, the greater understanding I will have in praying his will.

As I learn to pray, I realize that I have an enemy working hard to stop my interest in being in God's presence. There is raging at this moment a warfare in the heavenlies between the forces of heaven and hell. That fallen rebel who once sought to establish himself as God now moves ceaselessly throughout the earth, and aided by his loyal followers seeks to maintain control over my mind and heart.

God could choose to disarm and defeat the evil one, but he has sovereignly ordained that he would move through the means of prayer and fasting, to loose the chains of darkness, to tear down satanic strongholds and to release his supernatural power.

Prayer should be and become our first natural response to every circumstance of life. As I learn to ask and expect answers, sometimes my mind will follow another route with these questions: Why is it that God sometimes does not answer my prayers? Is the Bible not true in regard to prayer? Is it impossible for God to answer? The enemy is at work. Do I pray with a selfish purpose? I might ask according to his will but have an inner motive of my own gratification. I have to pray with the supreme nature to glorify Jesus (1 Corinthians 10:31). What I am praying for should glorify the Savior's name.

Do I pray with sin in my life? I might be praying God's will but I have sin in my life (Isaiah 59:1,2). God is holy and cannot be in the same breath with sin. Three is a separation that is necessary. I have to practice asking God if there is anything wrong in my life anywhere and to show me what it is, and I will give it up. He will make this known and then confession must take place (1 John 1:9). What is displeasing to God needs to be emptied out of my life.

Do I pray with idols in my heart? Idols will stop spiritual power in a person's life. An idol is anything I put before God: church, family, social position, job, education, reputation, power can all become idols. I must repent and change focus.

Do I pray with an unforgiving spirit? I have to search my heart and bring to light any enmity that may be in my heart toward anyone (Mark 11:25). Have I bitterness toward someone who has wronged me? Casting out any unforgiveness must take place if I am going to experience power. I believe praying releases God's power in my life when I am walking in intimacy with the Lord. A celebrated life involves prayer.

Dear Heavenly Father,

I am blessed to be able to come into your presence.
Help me to learn how to ask things for Jesus' sake.
Thank you for responding to my prayers. I live with
confidence because you are you, a mighty God that
hears.

I love you. Amen.

Personal Response

1. What has the chapter taught me? *(Overview)*

2. What level of commitment do I have in this study? *(Attitude)*

3. Who is my reliable resource? *(Confidence)*

4. What spiritual transformation have I learned? *(Discipleship)*

5. Have I experienced spiritual illumination? *(Enlightenment)*

6. What does the word "light" mean in this chapter? *(Understanding)*

7. Will I put the principal found in the chapter into prayer and practice it? *(Relationship)*

8. Will I share what I have learned in the chapter? *(Communication)*

CHAPTER SEVENTEEN

Intercession

JOHN 17:20

Life becomes a celebration as I learn to follow Jesus. Praying is a growing process. I started in my childhood. It has been an exciting journey to talk with my heavenly Father. Jesus Christ has paved the way and the Holy Spirit has brought understanding. I have shared insight into the disciples' prayer or Jesus model to follow. In it I discovered three forms of prayer which are petition, communion and intercession. I have looked at two responses to prayer: 1) I believe prayer brings me into God's presence; 2) I believe prayer releases God's power in my life. Now I am going to include: 3) I believe praying develops my fellowship with God; 4) I believe prayer requires my dependence on God. Each of these thoughts have led me into intercession for others in my prayer life. Jesus said, "Neither pray I for thee alone, but for them also which shall believe on me through their word." (John 17:20).

Praying is an essential part of my life. It is top priority. God has invited and encouraged me to enter into his presence and present his requests. I must seek him out in secret (Matthew 6:6). I must keep at it (Luke 18:1). I must come boldly to him (Hebrews 4:16).

Prayer is related to my worship (Matthew 6:9). I think that worship is the most important activity I can perform. God is worthy of all the praise and honor I can ever give to him. Almost every commandment and exhortation is fulfilled in worship as well as most of the promises. Indeed, "hallowed be thy name." (Matthew 6:9).

Praying is related to my faith (Matthew 21:22). Prayer is an expression of what I truly believe. I have to be fully surrendered to God if praying is a practice of what I believe. My will will be his will if I completely belong to him. Worship and faith are a result of that and obedience and desire.

Praying is related to my helper (Romans 8:26). Likewise the Spirit also helps my infirmities

. . . he maketh intercession for me. Prayer is a cooperative ministry and I am not alone. He is only a breath away. I am overwhelmed when I think of the Holy Spirit's participation in my life. When I cannot think and even respond., he is present helping me. I can go through any difficulty when I have this assurance.

Prayer is related to my intercession (Ephesians 6:18). I will persevere for the saints because he has called me to prayer. The people I come in contact with become my ministry of prayer. I was not designed to live an isolated life. I am a member of one body which is reflective in the local church. My interdependence is seen in the way I am dependent upon another through prayer.

Praying is related to the will of God (1 John 5:14). I have had to learn to mix the Word of God with faith. Learning to pray the will of God into actuality in my own life as well as others is an ongoing experience. My fellowship with God has grown. Prayer to God through his Son and the guidance of the Holy Spirit has brought sweet communion and intimacy with the supreme being. This is all possible through God's grace.

My effectiveness in prayer is based upon my dependence upon God. I am conscious of my need for him. Reliance is a daily thing that occupies my life. I do not start the day or end it without his presence. I realize that my existence is provided by the Almighty (Acts 17:28). Self-sufficiency is dissolved through a deep reliance.

I am learning that transparency in life before God's presence is needed. He needs not only my words but my thoughts and feelings. Any doubts or questions have to be brought to him. He wants me to confide in him and I must be open. Every part of my heart has to be transparent to the Lord.

Reliance and transparency leads to unwavering faith (James 1:5-8). A strong faith will produce a willingness on God's part to grant my petitions. I cannot live with a double mind. It is only one direction I have to follow. My divided allegiance cannot be in my life. Jesus Christ has to be Lord no matter what the cost. My life has to be characterized by a confident trust.

Unwavering faith, transparency and reliance need to be motivated by an intense fervor. I need to have determination in my prayer life. No matter what the circumstances, I have to practice wrestling with persistence. Then I have to, with confidence, leave the matter to the Lord and he will answer. Blessings from God will come when I obey God's way. A celebrated life involves intercession.

Dear Heavenly Father,
I am grateful Jesus Christ and the Holy Spirit intercede
for me. Help me to intercede for others.
I love you. Amen.

Personal Response

1. What has the chapter taught me? *(Overview)*

2. What level of commitment do I have in this study? *(Attitude)*

3. Who is my reliable resource? *(Confidence)*

4. What spiritual transformation have I learned? *(Discipleship)*

5. Have I experienced spiritual illumination? *(Enlightenment)*

6. What does the word "light" mean in this chapter? *(Understanding)*

7. Will I put the principal found in the chapter into prayer and practice it? *(Relationship)*

8. Will I share what I have learned in the chapter? *(Communication)*

CHAPTER EIGHTEEN

Denial

JOHN 18:25

Life becomes a celebration as I learn to follow Jesus. As I came to Chapter 18 of the Gospel of John, I discovered several topics to think about. Peter's words of denial, "I am not" would not leave my thoughts. At first I thought, how could he deny Jesus? He was close to the Lord. I know in my studies that the days Peter lived in were very difficult. It would take a lot of conviction, confidence and courage to stand up.

What about today? I could not help but join Peter in his weeping and sadness when he didn't have the strength to stand up for Jesus. How many times during a day do I fall short in being a good testimony for Jesus? I confess that I could be a better witness. There are times that I could say something but I don't. There are times I am embarrassed to say anything. There are times I just make excuses that are not valid. There are times I don't feel like it. There are times I think I don't have enough knowledge to defend the truth. There are other people that can do a better job. There are times I just think that I want to be accepted and not laughed at. There are times my own sensitivity gets in the way and I think the suffering is not worth it. I think there is too much of me in the way. Of course, the way of life today is "me-ism." I must refocus my thinking and I can become a fearless testimony for Jesus. I must claim the power of the Holy Spirit who dwells within me to produce the strength I need.

It has always been hard for me to open up and share even though I have many times in witnessing. Every ministry I have been in has brought new challenges. It is not dread or extreme fear that have followed me. It is because of my super-sensitive nature. Confrontation and debate with an agreeable taste is alright but when does that ever happen? I can disagree agreeably. I really have to rely upon 2 Timothy 1:7 which says, "God hath not given me the spirit of fear."

I am able to establish a daily bold witness through applying the text. To overcome personal weakness and inadequacies, I must be conscious of God's presence. If I am fearful, lack confidence or just uneasy, I must place myself into the text and share with the Holy Spirit who is my comforter. I have to claim the verse for every activity. I have to pray for the right opportunities to come to my attention. I must ask for God's courage and boldness. I must respond with love for Jesus Christ and be ready to glorify him. I must be sound in my judgement and be prepared with the strength of the Holy Spirit. When I lean on "the everlasting arm" of the Lord, the promise will be fulfilled.

I have seen it work in a variety of experiences. In music, I have created, developed and established many instrumental music education curricula. I have prayed for the right opportunity and through certain circumstances, they have opened up. When I started the programs at some of the schools, I was driving past the school and an inner voice (my subconscious) told me to stop and investigate the opportunity. I asked for courage and God's power and when I asked to talk with the administrator, he was already prepared for me. The administration and other officials had previously discussed the idea but did not know what step to take after that. I was able to establish the curriculum because God gave me a passion and love for music and children. I realized that students should have the right to glorify God in this way. I think the Lord gave me boldness to enter unknown territory because of the love he had produced in me. He also gave a sound mind and good judgement. The development of self-confidence through knowledge and previous preparations prepared the way. I did not have to enter into the opportunity with embarrassment because I was confident in what I was doing. God had promised the spirit of fearlessness. Power, strength, courage, boldness, love, passion, deep desire and a sound mind have been integrated together to bring success. "O how sweet to walk in this pilgrim way." It is fellowship with Jesus that makes it possible.

In ministry, this verse has paid big dividends. I was on the way to visit a family from my church because pastoral visitation was a worthwhile ministry in my church. I have always been organized and was following my agenda. This family was on the list to visit. As I traveled, I reached the top of the hill and came to a four-way stop. I had been praying for the right thing to talk about and would always leave a pastoral prescription with encouragement. My thoughts were deep in listening to the Lord. My spirit kept saying that I should turn left instead of right to the family's home. If I turned to the left, I would end up at the hospital. I didn't have anyone at the hospital to visit at this time. This would mess up my schedule, but the urge was so great that I was compelled to turn toward the hospital. I took an aggressive step and followed the inner voice.

When I reached the hospital, a nurse was waiting to direct me to a hospital room where a patient had asked for me. She was dying and was encouraged, by listening to a combined church music cantata that I had directed, to call for my presence. My visit was welcomed and spirit-led. After our visit, the Lord gave her peace and rest on her last few hours on earth. She would soon be in the very presence of her Savior. I was conscious of the Lord's presence. I was willing to follow whatever God wanted even if it didn't follow the previously prepared plan. I was in tune to his will. I walked into unknown territory without fear because the Holy Spirit was present with his power. I lost myself to the need of the hour and how could I be a servant to this dear lady that needed security and a sense of God's presence. I do not remember what was said but sound judgement and spiritual enlightenment was shared. The love of God was manifested and motivated my direction into this changed plan of action. The Lord does not give fear but confidence as we fulfill his plan and rely on Him. A celebrated life involves boldness and not denial.

Dear Heavenly Father,

Help me to affirm your promises. Help me to be dominated by the Holy Spirit. Help me to never deny

*you. Help me to live with your power, presence and
peace.*

I love you. Amen.

Personal Response

1. What has the chapter taught me? *(Overview)*

2. What level of commitment do I have in this
   study? *(Attitude)*

3. Who is my reliable resource? *(Confidence)*

4. What spiritual transformation have I learned? *(Discipleship)*

5. Have I experienced spiritual illumination? *(Enlightenment)*

6. What does the word "light" mean in this chapter? *(Understanding)*

7. Will I put the principal found in the chapter into prayer and practice it? *(Relationship)*

8. Will I share what I have learned in the chapter? *(Communication)*

CHAPTER NINETEEN

Crucifixion

JOHN 19:28

L ife becomes a celebration as I learn to follow Jesus. The Bible says, "Believe on the Lord Jesus Christ and thou shalt be saved . . ." (Acts 16:31). I have to believe that Jesus fulfills God's demands in that he bore my judgement on Calvary. (Romans 5:6-11; 2 Corinthians 5:21; 1 Peter 2:24). What I deserved fell upon him. I have been redeemed. Salvation is a relationship with the Son of God. (John 1:12; Acts 16:31).

God has provided in Jesus Christ and his sacrificial death a spiritual deliverance. He has provided life (Ephesians 2:5) for our death (Ephesians 2:1), forgiveness (Colossians 2:13), for our guilt (Romans 3:23), righteousness (Romans 8:3,4), for our unrighteousness (Romans 3:10), reconciliation (Ephesians 2:13-16), for our alienation (Ephesians 2:12), cleansing

(1 Corinthians 6:11) and for our depravity (1 Corinthians 6:9-10). The list is endless.

In the crucifixion, a provision for cleansing from the power of the old nature has been made (Romans 6:1-10). My sinful nature has been judged in the death of Jesus Christ. He was my representative. He took my nature to his cross so that I may be free from its influence. In his death, my old nature was stripped of its power. I have been crucified with Jesus Christ in his death. "I am crucified with Christ . . ." (Galatians 2:20). This means that I was crucified in and with him (Romans 6:1-10; Colossians 2:10-15, 3:1-3). The crucifixion is a historical event. I believe Jesus Christ died to free me from the power of my old nature.

I am saved to live with a new nature. I have to recognize that my old nature was crucified in the death of Jesus Christ. I am able to reject all its sinful characteristics. Through faith, I am able to receive cleansing in Jesus Christ. I may fall short and don't measure up to his standards, but I still have the power to win because he provided it. I have to make a decision to act in harmony with and on the basis of the atoning work of Christ. I legally died in and with Jesus Christ. The key word is "reckon" (Romans 6:11). In my salvation, I choose to put this principle into action. I can live free from the old nature. I must obey and forsake sin in my life. I have to trust God. This is a deliberate dependence on God for the grace necessary to practice my decisions. The decisions are not willful. It is a work of God in my belief. Without faith, it is impossible to please God (Hebrews 11:6).

I have believed and been saved. The crucifixion becomes real when I acknowledge my personal need, when I am specific in my confession, when I renounce the sin and when I receive Jesus as my cleansing.

Dear Heavenly Father,
With humble attitude, I come before you. I am thankful for your grace. I don't understand the full lostness of my soul or your suffering, but I have accepted the truth discovered in your son Jesus Christ. Thank you for being my substitute on the cross. I have

the assurance of sins forgiven and the acceptance of a
new life. Thank you.
I love you. Amen.

Personal Response

1. What has the chapter taught me? *(Overview)*

2. What level of commitment do I have in this study? *(Attitude)*

3. Who is my reliable resource? *(Confidence)*

4. What spiritual transformation have I learned? *(Discipleship)*

5. Have I experienced spiritual illumination? *(Enlightenment)*

6. What does the word "light" mean in this chapter? *(Understanding)*

7. Will I put the principal found in the chapter into prayer and practice it? *(Relationship)*

8. Will I share what I have learned in the chapter? *(Communication)*

CHAPTER TWENTY

Resurrection

JOHN 20:28

Life becomes a celebration as I learn to follow Jesus. Jesus' resurrection is involved in giving me enablement to live. His death takes place. He gives up his spirit. His body is placed in a garden tomb. Early on the first day of the week the tomb is empty. Jesus appears to Mary Magdalene and to his disciples. Jesus' resurrection provides divine enablement to obey God and to possess and to practice the virtues commanded in the Scripture. Those who do not practice the commandments and Word of God are not true believers (1 John 2:3-5). Obedience for God is equated with salvation (Hebrews 5:9) and forgiveness (1 Peter 1:2).

I am glad that through Jesus' resurrection that I can join Thomas (one of Jesus' disciples) and say, "My Lord and my God" (v.28). It is because of love that I obey (John 14:15,21,23). In the crucifixion, Jesus Christ provided a cleansing from my old nature. I am exhorted to "put off the old man" (Ephesians 4:22; Colossians 3:10). I have to learn to obey in this way. It takes a deliberate choice and practice. I have to learn to live in harmony with the resurrection (Romans 6:11).

I must also learn to live in the strength of the new nature (Romans 6:12). This involves active dependence on God. The resurrection power is found in the enablement. In Hebrews 13:20,21, I have found the blueprint. The authenticity is found in my Creator-Redeeemer. He is the author and dispenser of peace. I can trust my life to him. Peace is the result of that trust (May the God of peace). The blood that Christ shed on the cross secures God's promises for me. I rest on the decision of faith to rely on God's Word. His Word is power (blood of the eternal covenant). Jesus is the central focus. He is life because he conquered death. My enablement is through the power of the resurrection.

In my belief, I have access to the power of God (brought back from the dead). Jesus is the superior one. He is master (our Lord Jesus). Christ accomplished all his saving work for me. I have no needs he cannot meet. He will care for me better than anyone or anything (great Shepherd). God is preparing me and he will enable me for all I have to face (equip you with everything good). My duty is to please God through my good works. Under the new covenant, he will reveal his will. My will has to be willed to him (for doing his will and maybe work in us what is pleasing to him).

When I received salvation, I received all I needed. The emphasis is not on receiving but on development. It takes time, sacrifice, obedience, discipline, fellowship and trust (through Jesus Christ). I have life to participate in God's plan to bring honor to Jesus Christ. My Lord and Savior is Jesus Christ who deserves honor, glory, worship and praise. (To whom be glory forever and ever). This verse ends with Amen. It means "it is and shall be so." God will keep his promises and enable me to be all he wants me to be. His purposes will be established. I am able to focus my total being on Christ because of his resurrection. A celebrated life involves the resurrection.

Dear Heavenly Father,

Thank you for loving me. To comprehend your love is impossible and I am simply glad that you do. Please infuse me with your love. Help me to be motivated through love. You have many times used the word 'witness' in the gospel of John. I pray that your love will absorb me and I will be a witness of your great love.

I love you. Amen.

Personal Response

1. What has the chapter taught me? *(Overview)*

2. What level of commitment do I have in this study? *(Attitude)*

3. Who is my reliable resource? *(Confidence)*

4. What spiritual transformation have I learned? *(Discipleship)*

5. Have I experienced spiritual illumination? *(Enlightenment)*

6. What does the word "light" mean in this chapter? *(Understanding)*

7. Will I put the principal found in the chapter into prayer and practice it? *(Relationship)*

8. Will I share what I have learned in the chapter? *(Communication)*

CHAPTER TWENTY-ONE

Challenge

JOHN 21:15-17

The celebrated life includes the challenge of love. I have had to return to my childhood and sing, "Jesus Loves Me, this I know, for the Bible tells me so." The love of God is the greatest thing in the universe. The celebrated life includes the challenge of love. The Bible says, "But God, who is rich in mercy, out of the great love with which he loved us" (Ephesians 2:4). The word 'love' goes far beyond my own ideas. Love found in the Bible refers to general affection, friendship, sensual and sacrifice. His love for me is stupendous. It is way beyond my comprehension. I am assured of that kind of love. The Scripture says, "in the love of Christ which surpasses knowledge that you may be filled with all the fulness of God" (Ephesians 3:18,19). His love is infinite and cannot be exhausted. I cannot understand it but I am experiencing it.

A favorite verse in my childhood and senior years is God so loved (John 3:16). In his love, he gives the best of gifts. He has given himself. There is nothing that anyone can give greater than that. God gave himself in Jesus. I am assured of that kind of love. His love is also sovereign. He is free to love whom he chooses. He is not influenced by anything and his love lies only in himself. "He destined us in love to be his sons through Jesus Christ" (Ephesians 1:5,6). The final word description of love is eternal: "Who shall separate us from the love of Christ?" (Romans 8:35-39).

His love is found in eternity past and eternity future and has no end. Nothing can separate me from his love. God has decreed that it is only in Christ that his great, infinite, giving, sovereign and eternal love for sinners may be known. I am assured of his love. I am grateful for his love and for the infusion of that love in my own heart. Through Christ's sacrifice, death, resurrection, ascension and pentecost, I am complete.

As I have come to the last chapter of John's gospel and my book, I have reviewed

Peter's denial of Christ. I am reminded of the importance of love. Jesus says 'love' three times. He emphasizes the highest kind of love. He emphasizes intimacy, intensity and a deep relationship. He also emphasizes friendship and fondness. No matter the circumstance, I must fix my eyes on Jesus (Hebrews 12:1,2) and accept his love and give my priority to loving him. Jesus says, feed and care for my sheep (John 21:15,16) and supply food for them and disciple them through leadership and guidance. A celebrated life involves challenge.

Dear Heavenly Father,

Thank you for loving me. To comprehend your love is impossible and I am simply glad that you do. Please infuse me with your love. Help me to be motivated through love. You have many times used the word 'witness' in the gospel of John. I pray that your love will absorb me and I will be a witness of your great love. I love you. Amen.

Personal Response

1. What has the chapter taught me? *(Overview)*

2. What level of commitment do I have in this study? *(Attitude)*

3. Who is my reliable resource? *(Confidence)*

4. What spiritual transformation have I learned? *(Discipleship)*

5. Have I experienced spiritual illumination? *(Enlightenment)*

6. What does the word "light" mean in this chapter? *(Understanding)*

7. Will I put the principal found in the chapter into prayer and practice it? *(Relationship)*

8. Will I share what I have learned in the chapter? *(Communication)*

Conclusion

JOHN 7:37-38

"Jesus stood and said in a loud voice, "If anyone is thirsty, let him come to me and drink. Whoever believes in me, as the scripture has said, streams of living water will flow from within him."
—John 7:37-38

- My life in Jesus Christ is a life to celebrate. It all starts with activating God's word. As I apply God's principles in the Gospel of John, I will learn to pray with streams of living water within my heart produced by the Supreme Being.

- I want to allow Jesus Christ to live through me. Transforming power will do the work. Christianity is the indwelling of God into our everyday activities. I celebrate Jesus for the power flows within me.

- I want to communicate God to man. Belief gives the authority to place us into his family. I celebrate Jesus for communicating truth to me.
- I am developing a relationship with God through Jesus Christ. Quiet times of meditation has produced the way. I celebrate Jesus for complete sufficiency.
- I want to characterize Jesus. Internal change is taking place. Spiritual transformation is a new pattern of life. I celebrate Jesus for transformation through the sustainer.
- I am learning to worship with the right attitude. My guide is to worship with the Spirit of truth. Worship involves love, time, choice, sensitivity and God-consciousness. I celebrate Jesus for giving me opportunity to worship from the heart.
- I am responsible to respond. It all starts with belief. It involves faith. I celebrate Jesus for saving me from judgement and wrath.
- I am grateful that I have been chosen. I have been enslaved to sin. God has enabled me to

believe. I celebrate Jesus for giving me the gift of faith.

- I have been in the center of interpersonal tension. This has included growing in grace. I am yielded to divine control. I celebrate Jesus for helping me to be a peacemaker in conflict.

- I am thankful for who is in charge of justice. The word salvation means savior. I celebrate Jesus for deliverance and victory over sin and weakness.

- I am thankful for Jesus Christ's credentials. Many people ignore the evidence , causing them to decide to follow their own will.

- I celebrate Jesus that he is the light. Blindness is sad. Let God open the blindness to truth.

- I have a full and free life. Abundance belongs to me through faith. I celebrate Jesus for abundance.

- I see everyday emotion accompanied with sadness, anger, joy, sorrow, hate, love. Feelings are important. I celebrate Jesus for my reliance upon God's sensitivity.

- I am glad to praise God. I love the word "hallelujah." It has brought comfort, hope, love, etc. I celebrate Jesus through the privilege to praise.

- I have learned that love is a permanent badge of discipline and a foundation of unity. Love is submissiveness, active and constant. I want to infect others with the love of Jesus. I celebrate Jesus for his unconditional love. Genuine love is produced through the indwelling of the Holy Ghost.

- I have been comforted. Jesus has been the way, truth and life. I live with hope. I celebrate Jesus for comfort during suffering. I only have to apply the previous chapter.

- I have been experiencing remaining in Jesus. Loving Jesus will energize obedience to his commands. I celebrate Jesus as I present my spirit, soul and body to Jesus. It has to take place in that order.

- I have a helper. The Holy Spirit makes intercession for me. I celebrate Jesus because

I can pray to him. Prayer should be and become our first and natural response to every circumstance of life.

- I live in difficult days. Denial could be easy to admit for we live in a "me-ism" day. I celebrate Jesus and affirm his promises.

- I am thankful that my sinful nature has been judged in the death of Christ. Jesus' resurrection provides divine enablement. I celebrate Jesus that my new nature is developmental.

- I have received the best of . . . God has given himself. He gave himself in Jesus. His love is sovereign. I celebrate Jesus that his love will absorb me and infuses love into me.

Sources

- Boice, Montgomery James, *Foundations of the Christian Faith*, InterVarsity Press, 1986.
- Gillette, John F., *A Triplet's Trilogy*, J.F.G. Ministry Publication, 2006.
- McGee, J. Vernon, *Briefing the Bible*, Zondervan Publishing, 1949.
- Vaughan, Curtis, *The New Testament From 26 Translations*, Zondervan Publishing, 1967.

Acknowledgements

I appreciate all the people that God has used to influence me. Many of these thoughts have come to my memory over the past seventy-nine years through sermon notes, lectures, conversations, meditations and reading. I have not knowingly withheld any significant reference from others in my devotional. To the best of my knowledge, all statements and information are true and correct and given credit. Everyone I have come in contact with should be given credit. Pastoral Health Care and Divine Dialogue Series is a constant source of encouragement.

About the Author

 John F. Gillette's story started with a miracle. He was born a member of a trio — triplets. He has learned every moment needs to be in God's presence. His desire is to glorify the Lord Jesus Christ in health and in sickness. The Pastoral Health Care book series was created through unexpected heart disease (open heart surgery), cancer (medication and surgery), a stroke, brain bleeding, loss of hearing and the death of his wife that has caused much pain.

His studies and experience have provided a spiritual solution to suffering. His many years of Christian service include state certification in education and ordination in ministry. He earned a Doctor of Philosophy in Religion with the development of a local assembly. He was honored with a Doctor of Music in education after establishing fifty school music departments.

He was awarded a Doctor of Ministry in pastoral health care in creating a spiritual, psychological, and physiological adjustment for several organizations. A miracle in observing and obeying God's perspective on eternal values has taken place. He believes in God's sovereignty and compassion. He is learning to let go of self and to hold onto someone who can do whatever he pleases. The proclaiming of the sacred scripture has always been his motivation in music, ministry and mentoring. He has been driven by passion, independence and diversity. Pastoral Health Care has brought security. It may help you as well.

More Books in the Series:

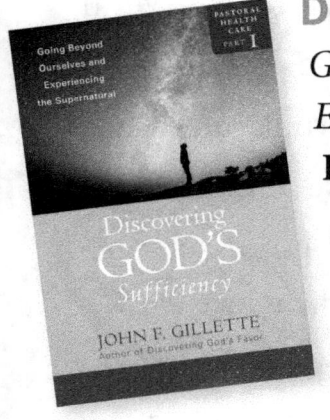

Discovering God's Sufficiency
Going Beyond Ourselves and Experiencing the Supernatural
Pastoral Health Care—Part One

Can anyone fix our troubles? The answer is 'yes.' How do we conquer our trials? We have to affirm God's intervention. We have to accept God's indwelling. We have to make some adjustments through God's illumination. We can experience God's power, presence and peace.

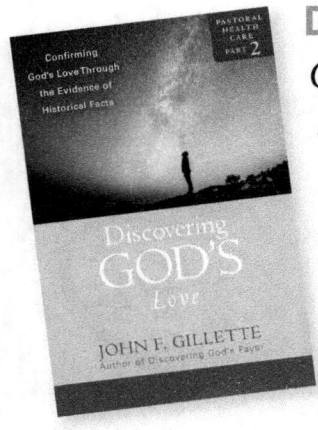

Discovering God's Love
Confirming God's love through the evidence of historical facts
Pastoral Health Care—Part Two

We can obtain strength to conquer through a knowledge of the 'Gospels' and receiving Jesus Christ into our hearts. The New Testament books of history give evidence of God's love. Through his love and faith, we are able to be strengthened, experience his support and become steadfast.

Discovering God's Counsel

Applying his spiritual solution to meet difficult trials

Pastoral Health Care—Part Three

Dark days can be life threatening. We have to develop an adequate level of spiritual, psychological and physiological adjustments. We can live with confidence in God's sufficiency.

Discovering God's Kingdom

Finding a way to understand ourselves in a complex world

Pastoral Health Care—Part Four

Dealing with life, death, heaven and eternity with God's perspective is necessary. It involves a personal decision of belief, trust and faith. Knowledge and commitment will bring comfort and security. The eternal destiny directive will provide the way.

Discovering God's Heart

Feeling God's heart pulse is our daily challenge

Pastoral Health Care—Part Five

We have to practice the principles in the pastoral health care meditation method. We can handle any situation through thinking biblically. The spirit, soul and body are involved. Therefore, a holistic approach has to take place.